The Street to Recovery

Kevin Kennedy

Paperbooks, The Old Fire Station, 140 Tabernacle Street,

London EC2A 4SD

info@legend-paperbooks.co.uk www.legendpress.co.uk

Print ISBN 978-1-9095936-3-3

Set in Times

Printed by Multiprint www.multiprint.bg

Main Cover Photography by Headshot London www.headshotlondon.co.uk

Cover design by Gudrun Jobst www.yotedesign.com

Photography © Ralf Brinkhoff, photo insert page 16 and cover (lb).

Coronation Street images © ITV Granada

Contents

Prologue: a Friday in early August, 1998

Sometime in the morning, I came round.

I'd blacked out from the drink, with no memory of the night before. As soon as I opened my eyes, before I'd even focused on the room around me, I knew I had done it again. After all the promises, even swearing on the Bible and all the pleas for second chances, I'd still gone ahead and lost it. The four hideous horsemen – shame, remorse, self-disgust, and, worst of them all, fear – had found me, again.

The sickening realisation that yet again I'd let down the people closest to me, flooded through me. Mentally I started a damage control survey. However, even though I hadn't worked anything out yet, one overpowering thought loomed up – I wasn't very far away from needing another drink, badly. I wasn't sure I'd be able to stand upright without one, but one thing I was certain about, was that I wouldn't be able to get out the front door if I didn't have something to drink. Now, before I did anything else and even though alcohol had got me into all this trouble, I started to work out where that first drink might come from. I knew that very shortly I would go into involuntary detox, which would not only be extremely unpleasant for me, but possibly be highly dangerous.

The clock was running, counting down to the moment when if I didn't get that drink, everything would go wrong.

I had to open my eyes. Where had I ended up? Would I even recognise it? My eyelids were sticky as I prised them apart, and I fumbled around for my glasses. I immediately realised – the first piece of good news, I wasn't in a prison cell or a stranger's house – that I was lying on the couch in my flat, the one I shared with Clare, my wife of two years. I'd bought the place after my first marriage broke down; it was ideal for me, quiet, private, and ordinary.

Time to assess the evening's damage. I looked down. I was dressed, and nothing seemed stained with blood, vomit, or worse. Another good sign. I was stinking with sweat and booze but a hot shower would sort that out. No injuries, nothing missing – another plus. I could get myself ready for work, and, even though I'd be getting desperate by then, if there was no booze in the house, I could stop off on the way to Granada to buy myself a bottle and nobody would be any the wiser.

But where was Clare? I had, more often than I was prepared to admit to myself, ended up on the couch, while

Clare stayed in our bedroom down the corridor. It usually went the same way; a drunken argument, something totally silly would start me off and then I just wouldn't let go, I'd be like a kid picking at a scab and it wouldn't be long before I'd either head out, or be sent out, onto the couch, sleeping it off on my own.

'Clare? Clare? Clare!'

No reply. Slowly, gingerly, I levered myself into a sitting position. The silence around me seemed deeper, more ominous, the echo giving its own answer. Clare wasn't just not answering, she wasn't there in the flat at all. Tellingly, her handbag wasn't in its usual place. I could always tell if there was someone in the flat with me and I knew deep down from the empty sound around me that this time she was gone for good. I was on my own, which I realised was bad news indeed.

I stood up, swaying slightly, the movement causing a surge in last night's booze to race around my bloodstream, and a sudden heat flushed into my head. A deep breath and I'd calmed myself down. I still had some booze in my system, so I would be able to function as a human being for about an hour, two max. I needed to top up my levels fast. How was I going to do this?

Other questions crowded their way into my throbbing head. What had I done? Why had Clare left? I looked about the room, hoping to find some clues about my activities during my blackout. Nothing on the floor, other than the stuff I'd expect to see there. Nobody else's clothes – I hadn't brought a drunk friend back to stay over, then. Nothing seemed broken, at least nothing left there that hadn't been cleared away.

Except on the coffee table. In the middle, like the remains of a bomb that had gone off in the night, was a twisted, empty cocaine wrap. I didn't remember anything about that. I stared at it for a long time, willing myself to recall where, how, why. Nothing came to me. I was surprised I even knew what it was, so I suppose there was a part of me – just not the conscious part – that remembered.

Also on the table was today's filming script left open with my lines highlighted, so I must have done some work either before I went out or when I came in. I looked at the lines and they were familiar; I thought about getting to work, about being okay to work today – even though I felt like the world was going to end soon if I didn't get a drink – and decided to learn them properly. I sat back down again and started to read; I was in the middle of filming some scenes with Eve Steele, who played Anne Malone, and I never liked to appear on set without knowing my lines, that was bad form.

The clock, always the clock. Less than two hours to go now, until things went wrong.

Aware that I was going to start running out of time, I

thought I'd see if I had hidden any booze about the house. I'd discovered, some years ago, that a little sip first thing in the morning could steady me. I'd been making myself a coffee one morning; I'd got up and felt really, really rough, and as I was going to work that morning I headed into the kitchen to make a strong coffee to perk me up. Someone had been to Jamaica or one of the Caribbean islands and they'd brought back with them a doll, a Jamaican lady with a bottle of rum inside. I started making my coffee, feeling pretty grim, and looked up from the cup to stare ahead of me and there on the shelf was the doll. I looked at it for a moment and then took it down. I unscrewed her head, poured some rum into the coffee and took a good sip. As the hot liquid burned its way down my throat it was like a revelation. I felt marvellous and the scales fell from my eyes – here was the answer to my problems in the morning.

That was the start of my secret drinking.

The rum in the doll didn't last too long, so I had started to bring bottles home and put them where I thought nobody else would find them. That morning I searched all my usual hiding places: I started with the fridge, checked on top, behind, but there was no joy. I went into our bedroom and looked under the bed – always a favourite – but nothing. I rummaged through the cupboards, the bin, at the back of the wardrobe, among the bags at the bottom of the wardrobe. I checked the pockets of my jackets, the insides of my shoes, under the sofa, behind the sofa. Still nothing.

I checked my hands – they weren't trembling yet, but I knew the shakes weren't far away. If I went without a drink any longer then my guts would start to tighten, like a tea towel twisted until it resembled a knotted rope. If that happens, it's almost impossible for me to keep anything down, and it's never a good idea to vomit on set. What I needed was alcohol to loosen the knot in my guts, to steady my hands and more importantly to stop my heart and my head from racing.

It's hard to describe to anyone who hasn't been through it but I found involuntary detox hell on earth, and the knowledge it was soon to start happening was something I dreaded. It's not just the physical effects I would go through, but the mental anguish, shame and wretchedness. When it kicked in, I knew I would feel as if I was the most tormented, loneliest person on earth. I knew right from wrong, I knew that I was only hurting myself, the people I loved and who loved me. I knew without having to even think about it for a moment that what I was doing was very wrong, but at that moment I had no choice, I had to have a drink or I risked being found out for the miserable excuse of a human being I really was.

I'd been through it once before, some years ago. It wasn't long after my Grandfather had died and I'd felt that as a tribute to him – he was a Royal Navy man – I'd like to take a short sea-voyage, so I signed up to travel from Falmouth to Pwllheli on board a three-mastered schooner, the *Black Knight*. Cleverly, I made sure I'd enjoy the voyage by getting plastered the night before in Falmouth, and staggered on board with bottles clinking in my luggage.

I hadn't reckoned on bad weather. Not only did I run out of booze fairly soon after we reached the Irish Sea, but we hit a really nasty gale as well. Here's where I was lucky – it was only because I was so horribly seasick that no-one found out I was going through my own alcohol withdrawal sickness.

I couldn't let that happen again, not now, not here. My alcoholic brain was going into overdrive and the desperate need to have a drink started to override all my thoughts: I need a drink, where can I get a drink, calm down, reassess the situation, I can't calm down, I need a drink to calm myself down, where can I get a drink – the circle was never-ending. I had been through this hundreds of times before. I thought it through carefully: right, so, there's no booze here, I'll have to go out and get some. I'll have to look as cool and nonchalant about it as possible. First thing, shave, take a shower, put some clean clothes on and prepare myself ready for work, regardless of the burning need inside me. I stumbled in the direction of the bathroom.

Looking back, it amazes me that I thought the shower had some magical healing powers, as if somehow the awful things I'd done could be washed away, the dirty water taking away all my secrets and all my problems down the drain – whereas in reality I would still be an addict, only just a cleaner addict.

Check the clock again.

Standing in the shower, trying to wash off the night before, my mind swirled round. What had I done? I can't say I wracked my brains because that would have hurt too much – I simply tried to retrace my path. Which pub had I gone too? Who was there? Could I recall any snippets of conversation, any remarks, jokes, anything that would trigger the whole evening to come rushing back into my memory?

The trouble was it could have been any one of a large number of places, where I'd ended up. I loved pubs, I always had done, ever since my mate Mike and I had tried to get our first drink in one, aged fifteen. We'd cobbled together about 14 pence each, which was enough to buy a pint of mild, and went in. It was a massive thing for any of us teenagers, then, being served our first drink in a pub; getting away with it meant something, then. I suppose I'd started when I was about thirteen, having a drink in the park with the others, but getting served in the pub was the thing – it meant we'd grown up.

It all stemmed from my Gran, God love her. She used to clean in a pub at the back of her house, just part-time work, and sometimes before I went to school, I was dropped off at her house because my mum had to go to work early. One day she took me into the pub as she cleaned it, before school started. I was very young but I remember thinking, what happens in this place? What goes on in here? There was a long wooden bar with a shiny brass rail that ran along the bottom of it that you could put your feet on; there were mirrors all around the walls that were polished until they gleamed, tall white handles for pulling the beer. I'd never seen this stuff anywhere else – it was like Aladdin's cave, only smelling of stale beer and old smoke. I was enchanted.

In those days pubs had frosted windows so passers-by couldn't see in, which only served to make it more mysterious and tempting to someone like me. Whenever I went past a pub, especially in the morning walk to school, the fans would be whirring away, extracting exotic smells and spreading them onto the street outside, and I'd think, I can't wait to get in there. Any kid would have been, because it was forbidden.

The real joy of the pub for me though wasn't the décor, the smell or even the booze. It was the camaraderie. It was unlike anything else I knew. I could go into a pub, and be like anyone else – someone who'd had a bad day at work, someone with troubles at home, someone with a great joke or a funny story to tell, someone looking for advice about cars or women, just a chat about football or politics – life was there, and once I was inside I could be like everyone else, and I'd be safe. That was what pubs became for me, a refuge from the outside, somewhere I could relax.

Standing in the shower, other thoughts crowded into my mind. More pressing for me though, almost as pressing as the need for a drink, was to try and figure out what had happened to Clare. I knew Clare had left, but I didn't know if she'd gone for good – although I immediately assumed the worst, as you do. I might have even spoken this thought out loud: this was it, end of.

Clare and I had been married for two years by now, and she was starting to get educated about my condition. She'd realised my drinking wasn't normal. We didn't regularly argue about it – well we did regularly argue about it, where I would say something inappropriate and it would cause friction and we'd get drawn into an argument entirely of my own design. We were party people, and we used to influence each other. She was my drinking buddy, and that's what we were about.

Her leaving me had been coming; too many of my second chances had been blown. I did remember that I'd gone out that afternoon to play some golf, but that never did happen. Obviously I'd gone for a drink with someone, and that had led on from there. When I'd finally made it home, there must have been an argument along the way, or Clare had taken one look at me when I staggered in and that was it. I had to imagine this is what happened – I had no idea.

I had ended up on the sofa before. Sometimes I'd started off in bed and there'd been a row and I ended up on the sofa. That was quite often, because like most drunks, I wouldn't leave it alone. You'd pick an argument and go back to it. If you were drunk, you'd pick it and pick it until it explodes. I was already pissed and that was just the devil in me. I wasn't sober ever, but I was affable. I could be vicious verbally, but never violent as far as I know. I was more annoying than anything. But no matter how hard I tried, I couldn't recall any kind of argument from the night before, or anything that might have led to me waking up in the wrong room.

I finished shaving and scrubbing myself free of the detritus and changed into some clean jeans and a t-shirt. Fifty minutes since I came round, it's going to be tight. I started to look at my lines again. The first scene was fine, the second one was almost there, and the third – well, it was only a few lines and I would get time later that morning to really cement them in.

Check the clock.

I looked back down at the pages in my hand and noticed that my hands were starting to shake. This was bad news because I was so self-conscious of shaking when handing over money for booze at the till; buying vodka at 9.30 in the morning didn't bother me at all, but having the shakes as I handed the money across wasn't a good idea.

I'd discovered early on in the first stages of addiction that a half-pint bottle of vodka, shaped like it is, is made for alcoholics because it's easy for them to hide one in their pocket. I always had my response ready, when I bought that early morning drink. So once I set off for work, I'd make sure that the route I took went past one of 'my' off-licences. That is, I'd made sure I knew the whereabouts of all the places I could buy booze on the way to work; I had a rota system going, so that I never went to the same place too often. I suppose you could say this was either paranoia at its most destructive, or great inventiveness on my part, depending on your point of view.

I'd park right outside so that I could rush in, making it seem as if I had forgotten something on the way to work. Usually it was 'a mate's birthday'. I'd pick up a card, get to the counter, look about in a slightly puzzled way, as if surprised to see drink in there, and say something along the lines of, 'I'm getting this for a friend's birthday – I haven't got time to get him a proper present – can you give me one of those small bottles of vodka there?' And I'd gesture towards the shelves behind. If I was challenged, that is, if the shopkeeper pointed out that it was way too early for them to be selling booze legally, I'd usually give them some spiel about being in a rush, that I'd forgotten it was my friend's birthday, that I really didn't want to see him without having something to press into his hand and that I wasn't aware of the licensing restrictions. This last ploy never failed.

It was important to me that I buy a half-pint. I never bought a full bottle, because that would be bad, that would be what an alcoholic bought, some of those guys I'd seen in the parks, swigging from a bottle on a bench. I wasn't one of them, an alcoholic like that, at least not in my eyes. I just needed a little bit of booze at that time of day to take the edge off, that was all.

Being an addict is something that no-one, those lucky people who've never been through the wringer themselves, can understand, as everything becomes secondary to the need for a drink. Take the moral question, the idea that we all of us know what's wrong or what's right. It's not that I lost sight of the differences between good and bad, but the overriding need in me for drink was incredible, and my brain would convince me there was a huge grey area in between. I was buying booze outside licensing hours, I was making the shopkeeper break the law by selling it to me, but this could be got round in my mind with words like 'just', or 'only', or 'this once'. I found I was manipulating myself – and everyone else – to get what I wanted.

My mind had wandered from reading my lines and I was

thinking about where my drink was going to come from.

Check the clock again.

I reckoned another half an hour and things would start to get nasty, I was already beginning to sweat in the early summer's heat, and despite the shower, I knew I would smell of yesterday's indulgences so as I looked for my car keys I made a mental note, aftershave and mints – lots of both. Then, disaster, no car keys. They weren't where I left them and I always – drunk or sober – put them in the same place.

Real panic started to set in. If I couldn't use the car, I couldn't get booze and if I couldn't get a drink then there was no way I could go to work, because I had to have that drink to be able to be normal and at work everything had to seem normal. If I got a taxi then the taxi driver would know my secret because I would have to stop at an off-licence and no matter what line I used to get the booze at that time of day, once I was back in the cab there was no way that I could hold on to that bottle and not take a swig from it. If I didn't have that drink before I got to Granada then I'd be too far in the grip of involuntary detox to be able to keep it down and I could hardly tell the cabbie I was drinking vodka at that time of day to toast my mate's birthday.

A lot of people think that being an alcoholic is an easy escape but it just brings with it a host of problems, all sorts of difficulties that take an unnecessary amount of time and energy to try and overcome. My brain would stop working logically, and be taken over by one burning desire that pulled all my strings – booze. Logic took a back seat then, and all normal decisions, plans, thoughts, all of them, went there too while I was gripped by this oppressive need for alcohol.

Once again I started my frantic searching. For the second time that morning I rummaged through drawers, opened wardrobes and bags, looked under beds, chairs and sofas, stuck my hands into endless pockets and scoured the surfaces of the kitchen, the table, anywhere I might have dropped the keys or where Clare might have chucked them in anger with me.

They were nowhere to be seen.

Check the clock.

Things were getting worse as the first of the stomach cramps hit me, bending me double as the waves of pain rolled through my insides. My anxiety – well it was more than that, my rising panic is what it was – was that I wouldn't be able to get that drink at all. Then what would I do?

Just then the doorbell rang. I nearly jumped out of my skin, my nerve endings the previous evening had been dulled from a nice coating of alcohol I'd poured on them, but now they were like exposed wires hanging out of a plug socket. Who the hell could this be? All morning I had been in total denial about my last bout of drinking, could this be a consequence – the police? Or worse, the press? Both of whom I'd been living in fear of for what seemed an age.

Every time the doorbell rang I thought that this would be some exposé from the papers, but thankfully it never happened. Once the *Mirror* came on to me, about me buying booze from a shop somewhere, but it turned out that the person who'd tipped them off was someone with a complaint against the shop and that was what the story was about, not me. I waffled to the editor, Piers Morgan, about buying the drink 'for a friend' and the story never ran. I'd known Piers for a while. One of my near neighbours, someone whose house I can see from my window, is Shaun Ryder; he called one day and said, 'I've got to have my photo in the paper, I've got the photographer here right now, would you come down and have your photo taken with me?' I wandered over and found it wasn't just the two of them, the interviewer, Piers Morgan, was there too. While we were having our pictures taken I started chatting to Piers and it came up that I was going to Dublin that weekend. We got on so well that Piers came along for the weekend too and we got totally wrecked – which he still talks about to this day – and ended up playing in a bar, a proper country music bar, called Bad Bob's in Temple Bar in Dublin, which I just loved. I've been friends with Piers ever since.

I knew though, that if Piers was given a story about me being an alcoholic, buying booze before going to work and drinking in secret, that he'd run it, friendship or no. Even though the press have been good to me in the past, on the whole, and even when some things they printed were way off the mark, I've always accepted it. To my way of thinking – and I've always thought this – you have to take the rough with the smooth. If you get into bed with these people, then sometimes it isn't going to go your way.

I unlocked my front door and pulled it open, carefully.

Standing there was a woman, late twenties, mousey-blonde hair, in a pair of jeans. She didn't look like a tabloid reporter, ready to fire questions at me. She had a look of concern on her face.

'Yes?' I managed to croak out.

'Hi Kevin, my name's Heather, I'm a friend of Clare's,' she said. I didn't respond, mostly because I didn't know what to say to this, I still wanted to know why she was there and when I was going to get a drink – it didn't look to me as if Heather was going to have one with her and so she carried on. 'Clare's asked me to come round and see if you were okay.'

Of course I am. I've had a shower, haven't I? I'm clean, aren't I? 'Yeah, er, yes, I'm ok,' I said. I stood back and held the door open wider, and added, 'Do you want to come in?'

Now I know to the reader it may seem boring that I'm always harping on about needing a drink, but if you think that's bad, imagine what it was like being me, when I needed that drink so badly. While one part of my mind was thinking nice thoughts – open the door, ask her in, don't know her but if she's a friend of Clare's, I should be polite, the other part of me was scheming – she must have driven here. She'll have a car. She can drive me to an off-licence and I can…'Clare asked me to come round,' said Heather, looking about her, 'because she was concerned about you.'

'Oh, yeah?' I didn't know what to say to this stranger about my wife not being there, but she seemed to know more than I did right now. I thought I should move on anyway so I patted my pockets as convincingly as I could, 'I seem to have misplaced my car keys… '

She interrupted me. 'Clare took them when she left. She didn't want you driving the car.'

'What?'

'Your keys. Clare's taken them.'

'What do you mean she's taken them?'

'She was worried about you.'

'Oh. Right, fine.' Nothing more for me to say on the matter, that was enough for now. I'd hoped to speak to Clare later on, after work, to find out what was happening. All that mattered at that moment was my getting what I needed. The situation was getting worse. My skin, as well as sweating buckets, was starting to itch and crawl, and I couldn't stop reaching up and scratching in irritation at the top of my head, as if somehow my hair was to blame for all this. Meanwhile my mind was working furiously, thinking of ways I could manipulate the situation without seeming fearful, without letting her know I'm withdrawing. 'Erm, I'm going to need to get a lift to work, did you drive over? Do you have a car? Can you take me to work?'

I daren't look at the clock, time had run out, my insides were tearing themselves apart, sweat was pouring from me and I was shaking violently.

Heather was talking to me but I wasn't listening. Fear and self-loathing was now replaced by a desperate physical need to get some booze, any kind of alcohol, inside me. I mumbled something about getting to work and eventually managed to steer this stranger down the stairs and outside to her car. I still wasn't listening; I was concentrating on walking straight rather than bent double, and how in hell I was going to broach the subject of an off-licence on the way to Granada.

If I'd been in a better state, I might have spotted that Heather didn't have a car, that she'd come over in Clare's Ford Fiesta, but I was so wrapped up in my own problems I didn't even notice.

Just as we got into the car, I told her, 'If it's alright with you I want to stop on the way for a paper.'

Heather turned to me and said, 'You don't have to hide what you're up to Kevin. I'm a member of Alcoholics Anonymous, that's one of the reasons Clare asked me to come down here this morning. If you want to get a drink, tell me.'

So I mumbled, 'Yes, alright, I do want a drink.' I didn't want to talk about Alcoholics Anonymous – nothing to do with me, I thought. We set off and I gave her directions, 'Take a left here, go that way,' steering her to one of my preferred shops. I was no easier inside, even though we were going somewhere that I could get a drink – I was still twitchy and sweaty. My nervousness started to grip me and as we drew closer, I started to worry – had she said that she was going to let me buy a drink just to get me in the car? She didn't seem to be slowing down, or looking to pull over at all. I was getting frantic, and started to kick off – 'If you're not going to stop then I'm just going to jump out, any moment,' I said. I grabbed the door handle. I was terrified but not because I was planning to jump out of a moving car and possibly cause myself some kind of injury, but because I thought she wouldn't stop – that's how bad I was.

Thank God she did.

With a rushed 'thanks' I almost ran into the shop while trying to keep the crippling cramps at bay as my body continued its withdrawal process. Once inside, I got either a quart or half-bottle of vodka, I don't know which, I just remember getting back into the car clutching the bottle. I swear as God is my witness as soon as I heard that *click* as I broke the seal I started to feel better. It had become one of my favourite sounds. I knew it promised comfort, and a respite from however bad I was feeling at the time. I've heard that drug addicts feel the same way when they've prepared their drug paraphernalia, but, thank goodness, that's one thing I never found out about from personal experience. All I know is that *click* calmed me down even before I'd had my first swig.

I brought the bottle to my lips – I didn't care that Heather was watching me now – and swallowed as much as I could as quickly as I could manage. The liquid hit my stomach as hard as an anvil as I downed the whole bottle with shaking hands. The relief was almost instant, my twisting guts began to unravel, I still had to fight to keep it down but it was too precious a cargo to lose now.

I drank the whole bottle down in one movement, a huge amount of vodka to have in one go. I remember everything, from the crack of the lid and the first gulp through to looking down at the empty end of the bottle. I didn't normally drink like that – that amount, in one go – and I knew I'd been lucky to keep it down. I suppose I really was at the end of my tether, sick and tired of being sick and tired, and I wanted oblivion, some escape from this whatever it was I was in. This hell.

Heather set off without another word in the direction of Granada studios. What happened next is something I've thought about ever since, I've analysed it, disbelieved, tried to rationalise it, but I still don't understand it and frankly I don't want to. Loudly and clearly, as if someone was sitting in the car alongside Heather – for some reason when I came back from the shop I'd clambered into the back seat of the car to down my delicious booze – said, 'You're going to die.' And it wasn't just any voice, it was my voice. My voice telling me this. So although I hadn't opened my mouth the words were spoken by me, out loud, to me.

It sounds simple in the retelling, but it was as if God himself had spoken to me, reached down and pulled the words out of my chest so that I couldn't avoid hearing them. 'You're going to die.' This moment of absolute clarity – that what I was doing was no way to live and for sure if I carried on I would die – hit me with such force that at that moment I surrendered, nothing else mattered anymore, not even Clare, my career, Coronation Street, family, nothing, nothing but stopping drinking and getting off this satanic merry-go-round.

Finally we arrived at the studios. Heather turned round to face me and said, 'We're here. What do you want to do?' but I had no reply for her, I couldn't muster the strength to speak at all. After a while, Heather got out of the car and went into the studios, leaving me in the back of the car, broken – I'm not sure that's even the right word, empty would be better. I sat there stunned, like I'd been hit by something. I knew this was my future unless I did something about it. It wasn't me being brave or anything like that. I was stunned by the truth of the situation I'd found myself in and the battle that morning, knowing I'd only got this amount of time – because I'd been through detox before, on the *Black Knight*, and I knew how awful that was going to be.

What I didn't know, though, was that while I'd been at home that morning – while I'd been worrying about how to keep my secret – wheels had been turning and Heather's appearance at my door was part of an orchestrated campaign.

Granada had tried to contact me earlier, in fact had been trying all morning. Although I'd spent hours earlier that day fretting about the clock, with my mind whirling away around the deadline I'd set myself for getting another drink inside me – even though this had been going on, I was still very, very late for work. I was due on set about 10am and I was always there in plenty of time for make-up and to make sure I had my lines down, I'd have been there at least before 8.00am usually. Heather had called for me about 9.00am, but I only know that now because I've asked since. I suppose the truth is that I was so far gone that I had no idea any more what was going on around me. Somehow I'd not noticed that Granada were after me – I must have switched my phone off, or dropped it, or any number of things – and in the end, getting slightly desperate, someone had asked the producer, Brian Park, to see if he could contact Clare.

Brian rang Clare and asked, 'Where's Kevin? He's late and he's never late.'

She said, 'I dunno, I've left him.'

'You… you've left him?'

'Yes, I've left him.'

Inevitably the next call Clare received from Granada was the press office calling, and they asked, 'What is going on? Where is Kevin?'

'I don't know where he is. I've left him, I don't live with him any more.'

Cue mass panic stations at Granada. Cue Clare ringing Heather, asking her to come and check on me, as she couldn't – wouldn't – come herself, but if no-one had seen me that morning then Clare was worried. She asked Heather to get me to Granada, if I was fit to go to work.

Things worsened once we arrived at the studios. I knew the game was up at this point, because Heather told me Granada were now involved and I refused point-blank to get out of the car. Heather tried to get me to go inside but I wouldn't. I was paralysed with fear, and remained stuck in the back seat where I wouldn't budge. I don't know what had happened, but everything had reacted with that moment of clarity and completely screwed me up, plus the alcohol just finished me off, and I was incapable of getting out of the car. I couldn't move. So she went inside to speak to someone and was shown into the producer's office.

After a while, Brian Park came out to look at me. Brian is a small, neat, sandy-haired man, and he was wearing a t-shirt that day, for some reason I can still picture that. The passenger door window was wide open and Brian stuck his head through to look at me in the back seat. He said something to me but I wasn't listening, I was too scared, I was absolutely petrified. I'd had to wait ages while Heather went in before Brian appeared, I was sat in this car on my own, and every moment I was left waiting seemed an eternity – the clock, which had been my enemy earlier, had now become an implacable foe. Brian tried to get me to move too but nothing seemed to register with me at all, so after speaking to Heather again he went off to talk to Clare once more.

I remember nothing of this. I have no recollection of the words Brian spoke to me, all that I can recall is the awful, overwhelming sense of terror that I felt. At that moment I knew just how much trouble I was in, a dreadful, dreadful place to be. If you'd asked me before what being rigid with fear meant I couldn't have told you, but I would have guessed that it would be how you'd feel if you were confronted with something frightening and threatening – a Great White Shark, perhaps, or a lion. Now I knew better. It didn't have to be a threat that you could see for it to be real, so although I couldn't tell you what shape my fear took – fear for my future, my career, my wife, my family, my life even, perhaps all of those and more – I was certain that it had me pinned down in the back of that car.

Brian Park had gone back to his office to phone Clare. He explained to her that I wouldn't get out of the car and that it was vital that she came down to help. Initially she refused, she had quite rightly had enough of my problems and – thanks to people like Heather – was coming to understand that you cannot help alcoholics in the same way that you can help others, you have to stand back and let them hit bottom so that you can pick them up.

Brian insisted Clare come in and finally she relented. Brian had told Clare that he'd seen me and was shocked at just how bad I seemed to be – 'he's in a terrible state, he's very poorly.' When she did arrive he explained to her exactly what they were going to do; that the studio had booked me into the Priory Hospital nearby, and that I was going to be taken there to recover properly – that this was to be no short-term 'drying-out' but the full package of rehabilitation. They were going to need Clare's assistance to get me there and that's why they needed her to come in to see me. Also, they had started to make plans to write me out of the storyline for a while; Curly was going to suddenly take it into his head that he wanted more than anything else to find out what had happened to Raquel, and would leave Weatherfield for six months while he went Down Under hunting for her.

As far as I know, this was the first time that's ever happened, for someone on Coronation Street to have been looked after that way. It's the American way – rehabilitation rather than sacking, and it has to be said it might be because they get back a better product, making it purely good business. Nevertheless, Brian Park saved my life, and I told him so and thanked him for it, when we met up many months later on.

Meanwhile, outside the studios, I remained very scared, sat in the back of the Ford Fiesta. One other person came out to see me, Corinne, the studio nurse. She knew what was going on with me, she'd come out when we drove up, taken one look at me (I hadn't noticed) and rushed back inside to start the process of getting me into the Priory. When she'd done that, Corinne came back outside to check on me. She's told me since that she knew what had been going on with me but that there was nothing that could be done, until I had realised for myself what state I was in and that I needed help.

Brian Park came back again and then things seemed to move very quickly; suddenly Clare was in the car next to me – although I had to be told this later, as it's another thing that I forgot as my conscious mind retreated so that I could only focus on what was going on inside me. We three sped towards the Priory in Hale, which is no more than twenty minutes away from the studios. It's another thing I have no memory of but I've been told that when we arrived, Heather and Clare went in search of two nurses who came and somehow managed to get me out of the car. They walked me between them toward the door, while I was screaming, crying, all at the same time, crying with desperation.

I suppose I knew, even though I was *non compos mentis,* that this was it: The End. Was it possibly the end of everything? As I was helped over the threshold and into the Priory Hospital, I could never have imagined that it was only The Beginning.

Chapter one: my brilliant childhood

I'm sure there are people reading this now thinking to themselves, Ah, I bet I know where his drinking started, it'll be because of problems in his youth. Well I'm sorry to disappoint anyone but I didn't have a bad childhood. On the contrary, I was very fortunate in my choice of parents and older sister. I came into a fully formed, warm and happy family environment. *Angela's Ashes* it wasn't.

I was born in Wythenshawe. Not the loveliest of areas, Wythenshawe has been, still is and will probably always remain, as rough as a bear's arse. We four lived on Greenbrow Road, a three-up-two-down house in the corner of a square with a big garden. I had a small tricycle, with whitewall wheels, that I pedalled round that square, in front of the house. When I'd finished racing, I'd play football, and the one and only time I kicked a ball through a window was at that house. My sister was nearly four years older than me, and she'd obviously used that time wisely, because she was then, and still is today, very clever. When I was seven, she passed her Eleven Plus, so I had that to worry about for the next few years.

My mum, Joan, was from a big family, one of six, so at my Gran's house there were always aunts, uncles, and cousins visiting or with us on our weekends and holidays away. There was Auntie Rose, Auntie Pat, Auntie Clare, Uncle Tony and Uncle Mike. They were all married, and every time I went to my Gran's it seemed another relative had arrived as she'd announce to my mum, 'Oh, your cousin's had a baby in Ireland.'

When Gran's house was full it wasn't so much lively as musical. Lying around the house amongst the books on plumbing – the men were busy learning trades – were stacks of sheet music. Everyone sang, Gran (who lived to 98) could play a mean blues harmonica, even though she had no teeth. My sister liked David Cassidy but played the French horn, while my uncles were in a marching and concert brass band. My uncle Tony had played in Shep's Banjo Boys, who appeared weekly on locally-filmed *The Comedians*, making him the first member of our family to appear on TV. One cousin, Chris Hook, was the band leader of The Temperance Seven and another cousin, Cush, went on to be in a band called The Men They Couldn't Hang.

Uncle Tony was also into his motorbikes, and, at the back of the garden, had a massive shed full of them. As well as a bar. Behind the shed was a hedge, and behind that, a pub called The Lantern, where, much later, I worked. Granddad got fed up of having to walk all the way round there from the front of the house and around the block, so he cut down the hedge, built a fence and put a gate in; all he had to do then was walk through the garden and across the pub car park.

Dad's family lived further away. Dad was close to his sister, and their mum lived in Hyde, on her own; Granddad had done a runner early on, and my dad never really knew him. He volunteered for the RAF, and he used to show me the scars on his legs and tell me that he'd got them 'putting out the fires on a burning Lancaster,' which even then I knew was total balls. He told me lots of stories like that, which always made me laugh. He dressed smartly for work; he worked for Northern Neon for a while, and then he got a job at Kelloggs, which he stayed in for a long time.

Mum worked for a firm who decided to move to Bedford; she didn't want to do that, to take her family away from Manchester, or to leave all her brothers and sisters and mum and dad. She decided this was an opportune time to pursue her dream of becoming a district nurse and as I grew up, there were textbooks everywhere as she studied.

Perhaps because of the overflow of books, when I was about eight or so we moved house. First we moved to Tamar Drive, to what we called the tin houses, because they had tin panelling outside, but the move was a disaster as we found the house was infested with fleas. Mum was horrified. We quickly moved again, this time to a brand new estate, called Tottenham Drive, which was still in Wythenshawe, but out west towards Altrincham. We were one of the first families to move in, the rest of it was still a building site. For a boy my age, it was the greatest place ever, an adventure playground on a scale I'd never seen before. There were no fences so I could wander through all the half-built houses, and, because it was still being built, the estate felt like it was in the countryside, with farms, country lanes, brooks to explore. Behind my house was a huge field, right next to the railway line, and on the other side of the railway line, there was another brand-new estate, which had just been finished.

My first school was Sacred Heart Primary School, where my sister had been, and which was just round the corner from my home. When we moved, I still went there. I liked Sacred Heart, it was a good Catholic school, and I remember it fondly, although I was always a bit scared of school as an institution. I didn't like the routine – I never liked any order – and I wasn't that keen on learning, either. The best thing about school was seeing my friends, and playtime, that's what I liked. To get to school once we moved I'd either walk with my sister, or get dropped off by my mum or dad, and afterwards I'd walk to Gran's.

She lived not far from the school and her house was pretty much the centre of everything, because all the kids used to gravitate there.

My family has strong Irish roots, and this would become increasingly more important to me as I grew older. There'd be evenings when the family, loads of them if not all of them would be round Gran's, and the stories would start. When I was little I didn't pay an awful lot of attention to what was being said over my head but as I grew up, I found some of these fascinating. At this early stage what I liked were the songs, I always liked songs that told a story. The evenings when the instruments came out after tea, and people sang songs, rebel songs I grew up with like 'The Merry Ploughboy' – they were the best.

At that age though, when they were just talking, I didn't want to be inside listening to adults, I wanted to be outside with my friends. Our estate had moved on from being a mere playground; people were more trusting back then and so there wasn't security all over the piles of bricks, the hills of sand. They all became part of a new landscape, ever-changing as our games dictated. What had once been something to run up and down on, or to climb, or to slide down now became ramparts to defend or trenches to take. We replayed the battles of Waterloo, Rorke's Drift, the Somme, Gallipoli, even Thermopylae on a weekly basis. We never broke anything, at least never on purpose, and if we weren't on the building sites, we were playing in the park next to the site, where we had the best game of them all – football. That space became our Wembley, our San Siro. I'd be Bobby Charlton when I was little, and then I wanted to be Joe Royle. I was becoming a City fan, even though my Dad leant more toward United. Michael Galway was my best friend then, and the two of us would spend all day out there. His dad Terry was a passionate City fan and he ran the local youth club, in the hall by Sacred Heart.

Michael Galway lived in the new estate on the other side of the railway tracks from me. We both had blue Choppers and we became thick as thieves. I spent half my life at his house in those days. My parents knew I was alright, as long as I was in by the time it was dark, they were fine. The exception was of course Bonfire night, when we boys built bonfires. One year on November 4th we'd scoured the area miles around for wood to make our fire the biggest there was, and then slept in it to stop people setting it alight. Today that would be thought extremely dangerous but we didn't worry about such things then, no-one did.

We went on our first trip abroad when I was about ten. Mum and Dad took us to Spain, I'd never been on a plane before and I remember that whole experience vividly. My teacher at the time gave me a bar of chocolate, why I don't know – did she think they didn't have chocolate in Spain?

Perhaps she thought I'd be frightened on the flight and need something to distract me. She needn't have worried, I was excited from the moment we arrived at the airport, as everything was different, and, to my young eyes, glamorous. First I had to go and see the huge iron memorial to Alcock and Brown, who'd made the first transatlantic flight in 1919 and who both came from Manchester. Then we boarded our plane, a Dan Air Comet. I wasn't going to forget that as the company's logo was stitched on to the back of the seat in front of me. If I leant to the side and peered all the way down the aisle, I could see all the way down into the cockpit. For a small boy, every part of the day was a great adventure.

For some reason, it was the middle of the night; maybe the flights were cheaper, no-one thought to explain that to me. I wouldn't have cared anyway. The moment the plane doors opened, and I stood on the top of the staircase, I was transported. It smelled differently to Manchester, almost a chocolatey smell (I'd eaten my chocolate bar ages ago). And, although it was night-time, it was still very warm. 'Mum,' I said, looking up at her, 'This is *amazing*.'

Mum and Dad had been abroad before so none of this was a surprise to them. Everything to me though was something I'd never seen or experienced before, and I soaked it all up as if I'd never get the chance again. From the luggage belt that moved, to the Spanish-speaking guide on our coach, which drove on the wrong side of the road but nobody minded, to the white street lights (ours were yellowy-orange at home), the motorbikes that seemed to be *everywhere* and then – our hotel.

We were staying in Lloret de Mar. We didn't unpack, we went straight to bed and even though I was exhausted I didn't want to sleep, but somehow I slipped into oblivion. I woke up in a start, suddenly in this incredible new world, with all my family there too, including my grandparents, the whole family had come out on holiday together. Granddad – as were all my uncles – was in the building trade, and they'd stop and look at Spanish building works (there was a lot of building work going on) and point and laugh. 'What a complete bodge job,' one of them would say. The nudges, whenever we went out, 'Look at the state of that.' We all ate breakfast together; Dad was working at Kellogg's and, for some reason only known to himself, brought some Corn Flakes with him and put that on the table every morning. Every morning he'd eat breakfast from his own box of Corn Flakes.

The hotel had a swimming pool on the roof, which we all thought was brilliant, especially as it was *properly* hot, and it had a slide. I learned to swim in that pool, like a fish. Mum always insisted that we learn to swim, she had a morbid fear of drowning. I didn't get any lessons or anything, it was do-or-drown, and, as I was forever in the pool, I just picked it up. I was like a straight line in those days anyway, quite long and lanky, and I really took to swimming.

In the evenings we'd all get together, go out and eat, where again everything was new, and crusty bread came with everything. Once, we ate paella and that night, Dad – who'd discovered a love for Sangria – brought back to our room from the restaurant a bottle of Coca-Cola that he'd filled with Sangria, so that he could have some later. I woke up in the night, dying of thirst, and I saw this Coca-Cola bottle. I picked it up, drained it and was pretty spectacularly sick everywhere, paella and sangria all over the shop. I've never been keen on fish since.

I came back home to Manchester with a new ability to swim, some sunburn, a big fluffy donkey, an even bigger sombrero and a secret interest in the effects of sangria. Package holidays in the early seventies were a fairly new thing and I'm forever grateful for my mum and dad for that first taste of 'Abroad', as it made a real difference to my outlook in life. When I take my own family, I explain to them it's not just about having a holiday as I point the different things out, it's also a good piece of grounding. Travel broadens the mind, we're told. It certainly did for me.

I was in my last year at Sacred Heart. I made my first communion and confession, along with all the pomp and ceremony that goes with that, wearing a red dickie bow.

The big thing that autumn was coming up to Mr Banion's class. Mr Banion was the Head and I wasn't looking forward to going into his class, I was scared to death of him. He represented the last stage of school, the Eleven Plus; my sister had sailed through hers and gone to a fairly flash school as a result. It would soon be my turn, and I was not in my sister's league, I was a bit slow on the academic side. I didn't like maths, and I didn't like reading; at least, according to my mum and dad, until the time they started showing 'interesting' foreign films on the TV. The screen would fill with subtitles and I would get frustrated: 'What's that say? What's that say?' It would drive me mad that I didn't know what the actors were saying, my parents think that's how I began to learn to read, but I think that's just folklore. I remained useless at maths, and that added to my terror about being in this class because that was Mr Banion's subject, along with RE, and those two together used to scare the hell out of me. His God was a God of fire and destruction, something of the times I suppose but I never liked sitting there listening to this – if you did wrong something would happen to you – it was proper Old Testament fire-and-brimstone stuff. Mr Banion took us through The Ten Commandments, talking about not worshipping false gods, and he said, 'If you decide to stay in your bed on a Sunday morning instead of going to Church, then you're worshipping your bed, not God. And that's a false god – your bed.'

At the weekends we went to church. All of my friends were Catholics and they went as well; in those days, we just did. Mum said to me, 'When you get to sixteen you can make your own mind up,' which I did – I stopped going. I quite enjoyed the Bible stories, but nothing else. While I was at school they built the church next door to Sacred Heart; there was always a Build-a-Brick appeal and it was immense, this big push to build the church. Then it was finally built, which was great because then they could stop going on about it. The seats were so uncomfortable, they dug into the back of your spine, I hated that. You couldn't get comfortable, no matter how hard you tried, and when you had wedged yourself in nicely, then it was time to stand up, or kneel down, up and down. I had no interest in it whatsoever. I'd known from the age of eleven that once I reached to sixteen I wasn't going to church again, ever. I could never get up for morning mass, which meant that I had to go to the evening service, which started at five-thirty, the worst possible time, because that was when the good kids' telly was starting. I harboured dreadful resentment against Catholicism, because I was missing children's TV on a Sunday. I really didn't like that.

One other thing stood out for me that final year: my sporting ability. All those hours in the pool in Spain had paid off. Every Wednesday, we'd traipse out (in all weathers) to the swimming pool with Mr Banion to race. I was fast. I knew I could beat everyone hands down. I liked that feeling of really excelling at something. Swimming became a big thing with me in those years. I passed all my badges, the short, medium and long distance ones, as well as the life-saving ones, which were very exciting and entailed jumping off the highest diving board in my pyjamas, taking off those pyjamas underwater, and diving down to retrieve bricks from the bottom of the pool.

In my school report for that year Mr Banion wrote, 'Kevin is going to be a future comedian'. That's an impressive observation considering I was only eleven. Making people laugh was my coping mechanism from my dislike of studying and my consequent failure. I didn't face the usual comedian's school-day enemy, the bully; I was blessed, I never came across bullies, and I was always up for a fight, I never shied away, always scrapping. I was very provocative as a child, quite feisty. I was always breaking my glasses, always losing them, I was a bit wild, but then, I was a little boy.

It was about this time that we got a new headmaster, Mr Sands, who as it turned out was very much into school plays. He decided that our year would put on an annual Christmas concert and an Easter concert. For the first one he made all our year stand up on benches and sing songs while he played the piano. Because I was thought to be musical, I was put in charge of the glockenspiel at one point, which was great. I used to like the build-up, coming up to showtime, all the mums and dads were there. We played the recorder as well. We had the school fair straight afterwards. It was weird seeing your teachers being more human. I enjoyed the singing, but I was making up the numbers. I'd discovered something else though, I enjoyed the performance – the buzz.

When it came to the Eleven Plus, I knew I'd fail miserably, I've never been good with exams. I got into St Paul's Roman Catholic School, which had a bit of a reputation. If I'd passed the exam, I'd have gone to Manchester Grammar – which was something else as a school – but that was not going to happen. In the mornings, my sister would no longer walk me to school; we'd leave home together, and walk round the railway, up past Timpson's, opposite Sacred Heart to the bus stop. My sister would get her bus going one way, and I'd get mine going the other way. Almost, as if in life.

On our first day, our teacher, Mr Ratterjack, who was Polish, drew our timetable on the board. I was terrified and thought it was some sort of test and that in copying it down I'd made mistakes. We all sat at our little single desks. I became friends with Michael Dunkley, who was a shy lad but very bright. Maybe, I thought, he's like me, a late developer – I'd heard adults using this phrase about me. In a different class, was Michael Galway, who was my very good pal, and in his class, Ray Kavanagh and Simon Bradshaw (Simon's dad was the Rural Science teacher, a lovely guy and a brilliant teacher). We'd meet up in the playground and this sort of gang began to form.

Me, Michael and Simon would ride to school on our bikes everyday, in all weather. Racing bikes, that is – we didn't ride the Choppers into school as they'd probably be nicked. Me and Mike would hang around on our Choppers on the estate all weekend.

In our first term, we were all sent to some other school, a rougher school than ours, for some sort of induction or other. Ray was with us and he was a lanky ginger-haired lad, very shy and this bully of a boy made a big mistake of picking on Ray. Ray didn't look much, but he was very hard and he just wiped the floor with the bully. Ray was a lovely bloke with a wickedly dry sense of humour. He was also a great footballer. We all played for our school football team, I was full-back. I wasn't a great athlete but I made up for that with enthusiasm. I was pretty shite, actually, but I did my best, and I got into all the teams so I must have been half-right. We had a team that did really well, and won anything; me, the two Michael's and Simon were in that. Michael Galway's dad, Terry, would come up to the sidelines and act as an unofficial coach. At half-time he'd come on and give the team talk instead of the teacher, Mr Smith – who everyone was terrified of. Mr Smith was a tall, imposing bloke, who you could hear coming for miles because of the metal caps on his shoes. He used to call people 'dumbos' and everyone had a natural hatred for him, me included. I met him years later, he was a very nice guy.

I had started following Manchester City at a young age, and all the other lads were City fans. It didn't take me long to get the bug badly enough to start disobeying my mum, which I felt bad about. Mum had forbidden me from going to the home games because of the heavy football violence at the time.

In February 1976, Manchester City reached Wembley for the League Cup Final. City were to play Newcastle. We'd beaten United 4-0 on the way to getting there. The only way I could get a ticket for the game was to collect vouchers. I was desperate to go. Mum and Dad still didn't know I was going to home games but of course they discovered my secret and Mum was not surprisingly cross with me. Dad talked her round: 'Look, he's going with his mates, it's not as if he's on his own.' However, I didn't quite have enough vouchers. Mum watched me sticking my vouchers in every night, got a stamp for me to post when I had to send it off and was with me when I got a reply back – *sorry*, it read, *you've not got enough vouchers* – half of Manchester had tried to buy a ticket. I was heartbroken because all my mates had tickets. Mum and

Dad must have had a conversation because one lunchtime outside school, Dad pulled up in his van and produced a ticket that he'd paid £15 or £20 for – a sum I had no hope of making – and I had a ticket.

Michael Dunkley and I went down on the coach that left at quarter past seven in the morning from outside our local newsagents. Mum fussed over me, going to London for the first time: 'Put your ticket in your sock, write the number of the bus down on a piece of paper, put that in your sock too.' But she needn't have worried, we had a great day out. City won the cup, beating Newcastle 2-1 and I'd never seen anything as big as Wembley in my life. 100,000 were there that afternoon. I returned home safe, hoarse and happy.

I now loved school, adored it, because of my friends, and the lessons themselves started to make sense. I was particularly interested in history; I was still useless at maths, and I didn't like French, I learned just one phrase: *Je ne comprend pas*. You could get away with that, for a certain length of time. I started to question religion: Mr Ratterjack told my mum that 'Kevin's *strongly* going to become an atheist,' and she wasn't happy about that. Mind you, I questioned everything. Erich von Däniken's *Chariots of the Gods* had come out, and I found what he had to say about the origins of religions fascinating. I also noticed something else; Dad was excused from going to church, and I wasn't. But all the boys went, and there was a bit of camaraderie in that. I also started to try a few different things.

At Gran's, I took up my Auntie Annie's guitar. I'd been encouraged to play from a young age but it was only at school that I really started to play. My own first guitar was a knackered Spanish one, the bridge was really high and the strings were like washing lines, very difficult to press down upon. But I persevered and, as Mum and Dad could see I was really trying, guitar lessons at school began. My teacher was called Mr Pegg, who knew my uncles; he had really long nails, to 'pick' the strings, as he also taught classical guitar. He taught me 'Greensleeves', even though I could never read music like that easily. I liked it, but I wanted to learn more progressive stuff, more tricks. Every guitarist does – how'd you get that sound, how'd you do this. I wanted to learn more. Mr Pegg was brilliant and encouraged me, he taught me a few chords, and that was the big one; I'd play a chord to try to work out the hit of the day. I couldn't afford music books, but I needed to know the right chord, so I would go to the music shops, find the right book, realise the missing chord, run back home and play it. I could play all the 'Kumbaya' stuff because that was just three chords, that was pretty easy. The first hit I tried to learn was 'Hotel California'. I got the first bit off, but the second chord – I struggled with that for a while before it was back down the shop again.

Michael Galway wasn't so interested in guitars but he and I were like brothers, I was always at his house. He had a massive double bed and we'd sit and watch TV in his room, and Mrs Galway – Sheila – would bring up food to us. Later on, when I started smoking, I could smoke at Sheila's house, I could even bum fags off her.

If I'm making it sound like I spent all my time doing the wrong thing, sneaking around my parents, smoking, then that's not what was really going on. I wasn't a bad child, I wasn't even naughty, not really. I had my moments, as any kid did, but I wasn't constantly badly behaved, not at all. I was a boy. I did things that boys do, but nothing that would point to being some sort of delinquent. There were a lot of boys just like me at that school. I was happy doing what I was doing and I had no plans for more mischief or anything like that. Talk about living in the day – I had no vision at all.

One thing I was doing that seemed to have half an eye on the future was acting. Acting started at school. We had a drama teacher at St Paul's, Peter Wells, who really encouraged me. I became interested in pretty much anything performance led, it was the first time I ever became aware of this. I wasn't shy. If I was told to be a tree, I'd be a tree. But I was also a bit of a clown at this point anyway. I was always up for a laugh – if I could make being a tree funny, then I'd do it. I was a clown, always one with the smart remark, an endless supply of stupid jokes. If someone dared me to do something then I'd do it. I liked the reaction. Whoever was watching seemed to like what I did, it was inevitable that I began to enjoy the showing-off bit of it, and I began to be good at it. Mr Wells saw I was teachable, I was receptive, so he put me into a bit of a play – and I thoroughly enjoyed it. I used to really enjoy the drama classes as Mr Wells could see that underneath the jokey bullshit I protected myself with there was a germ of something there.

What was I protecting? Apart from the never-ending quest to be liked, to be popular? Any indication of fear, I suppose, a fear of something I kept hidden. I hid it because who'd have cared – after all, what could I have to be worried about, let's be honest; I had loving parents and a great older sister; I had aunts, uncles, cousins who'd all have helped me out if I had a problem. I had good friends. I was never in serious trouble at school, and, while I was never going to be academic enough to follow in my sister's footsteps, I was not going to end up with nothing either. Maybe this was my problem; I was afraid of something, and whatever it was I'd kept it so hidden I couldn't even identify it myself.

At the end of every term there would be a bit of a concert. Mr Wells and Mr Ratterjack formed a panel to assess the acts that had volunteered, a sort of early Pop Idol/ X Factor set-up, and they decided I'd help them out. Why me? I was probably the only one who showed an interest in organising things, everyone else who wanted to perform wanted to be on stage, but I saw some possibilities here they hadn't seen. My classmates came along to audition: the first act was Tom from 3a, he was going to sing a song; then we had Katherine from 4a, she was going to do some juggling; next we had our girls from 5a who were going to be the Bay City Rollers. Michael Dunkley and I said we would do the argument sketch from Monty Python. Looking back, it was probably quite advanced at that age to go on a school stage and do that. To finish we had Marie from 5a, who was going to play the piano.

'Well,' I said to the teachers, 'how are we going to link all these together? We've got to fill the time while the people get on and off stage. Why don't I stand over there, like an MC?' I'd noticed that when Bruce Forsyth was on the 'Generation Game' he broke up the pieces by telling jokes, to keep things moving on and to soften the audience up. Mr Wells helped me write the links in the end; we used a joke book I'd bought, and he let me get away with taking the mickey out of some of the teachers. I can only think he let me because he was impressed that I had the balls to do so, at my age.

The pupils loved my linking bits, I said things standing

on stage with a microphone that I'd never have got away with in a playground – that was a lesson not lost on me. Everyone in the whole school knew exactly what I was doing, for instance, when I mimicked our headmaster, Mr O'Neill. He was a character all unto himself. He had one arm of his glasses missing, making them wobble about on his face; he wore a strange green suit, and he used to bounce up the stairs on to the stage for assembly. To use a microphone he'd do the same thing every time: he'd tap on it, saying 'one-two, one-two', as he did so. It was comedy genius, just there. I wore glasses myself, and being a kid, loads of my specs were broken, so I slipped a pair on, tilted them awkwardly, banged on the mic and said 'one-two one-two you dumbos'. The reaction was immense and I thought, Oh, this is good.

Church continued to play a big role in my childhood, even if I wasn't religious. I couldn't escape it at school, it being a Catholic school, I couldn't escape it at weekends when I had to go there and I couldn't even escape it in the summer holidays, when me and my friends were packed off by our families to some camp run for boys in Llanrug in Wales, run by the Brothers of St Vincent de Paul. Some of those Brothers were great – some were not. There were eight boys to a tent, I had just enough pals in our gang for us to fit in one tent with no room for anyone else. We'd go for a week every August. The Brothers aimed to get us physically exhausted and so we walked everywhere, we went canoeing, clambering up and sliding down mountains, that sort of thing. We all ate as much as we could at breakfast because that was the best meal; after that, it was just Spam served any which way. For our last day, we were taken to Llandudno for the day. We went on a train that took us to the Great Orme, the headland there. At the top there was a pub and with the encouragement of the Brothers we all tried cider, and then we were all sick on the way back down again.

School sent us off on a religious retreat, again just the boys, to a large house in the Lake District. We didn't get to have any fun this time, we just had boring classes about Catholicism. On the last night, we were told we could have beer with the meal, but before we were served any, we had a talk from this old bloke, an alcoholic. He stood up and – as I realise it now – did his 'share'. I suppose they'd brought him in from AA to do this talk. He told his story, about what booze had taken from him. I of course was the idiot who took the mick, saying to the other boys that the guy obviously couldn't hold his drink. When the beer came round, I drank mine and drank as much as I could of anyone else's – if they didn't want it, give it to me – almost as a reaction to what he said.

Back at home I was asked to play my guitar in the church. They had introduced 'folk' masses at church to make it less boring for people like me, I suppose, and as I was known to be able to play I was brought in. It was all 'Kumbaya' and stuff like that. I wasn't worried about playing, I knew I could do that, there were enough musical evenings in my family for me to know that; and I wasn't worried about playing in public. There were good bits and bad bits to being asked to do this. The good bits were I got to play and got the buzz out of a bit of a performance. The bad bit was I was right up at the front of the church, practically on the altar, so there was no chance of getting away with a bit of fidgeting, or falling asleep, and definitely no messing about.

Another boy I knew also turned up to play. He lived on the other side of the tracks, on the same estate as Michael, and I'd played a bit of football with him. His name was Johnny Marr, and it's almost pointless to say how good he was, even then.

Johnny said to me one day, 'I've got an electric guitar. Why don't you come round to have a look?' Now an electric guitar was a very cool thing indeed, so I eagerly turned up at his house with my guitar and we went up to his bedroom.

On the walls of his room he had a Manchester City poster, of course, and others of Thin Lizzy and Rory Gallagher. I knew about Thin Lizzy and I liked them, only I hadn't heard of Rory Gallagher; but when Johnny played me some tracks I quickly became a massive fan. He was one of the greatest guitarists that I've ever heard. Johnny showed me his guitar, a Stratocaster copy that he'd worked on to make it as much like Rory Gallagher's as he could. I sat on his bed ready to play some tunes with him, while he plugged in his Strat and he started playing. I was amazed – I didn't think anyone of our age could play like that. Even then, I just knew that this guy was going to be something special and that I was privileged to be the first person ever to play with Johnny like that. He was brilliant, melodic, skilful and fast. I thought that this guy was something else, and not only that, a thoroughly nice bloke. That jam session changed things, even more so when Johnny suggested we form a band. I had to get an electric guitar of my own, so I could play along properly with Johnny. Michael Galway was starting to get really into Deep Purple (which I never really understood because what's the point of getting into a band you'll never see live?) while Michael Dunkley was into Sparks. Michael Dunkley and I went into a music shop in Altrincham where we saw two guitars, a bass guitar and a rhythm guitar, that we wanted. Both had red bodies – horrible things they were – but they were affordable, and we asked if we could begin putting money down every week for them. The shop manager said, 'You can do that or instead, why don't you come and work Saturdays for me?' So we spent our Saturdays cleaning drum kits with ammonia, to work off the debt for the guitars. We also found another place where the owner wanted the room above the shop painted, so we set to painting a room and the fumes were incredible. There was a sash window and as I pushed the sash up to let some air in, it came banging down and the window broke, crashing glass into the street below. And that was the end of that job.

The music shop used to be a newsagents and one day, Mike and I found a load of bangers that obviously had been in the stock of the shop. We stole them and that summer night (it wasn't the season for loud explosions) the two of us biked round Wythenshawe, pursued by the police, blowing them up in phone boxes, post boxes, old ladies' flats, underneath cars, bikes, bushes. We were never caught.

Finally, we had enough money for the guitars and Mike and I took them home to start playing. My dad bought me an amp to play it through, a VOX AC30, a valve amp, the kind the Beatles used to play. Johnny had found a drummer, a boy living opposite, called Bobby Durkin. He also came up with a name for us, The Paris Valentinos. I liked that. I was going to be in a band, wow.

To be honest, it wasn't so much of a band as a social thing; we only really played one gig, which was a Jubilee street party, and we'd only practiced about three songs: we played 'Anything That's Rock'n'Roll' by Tom Petty, Rory Gallagher's 'Shadowplay', and a very slow version of 'Don't Believe a Word' by Thin Lizzy. We had some tables pushed together and though the nucleus was the three of us, we also had a singer, I can't remember his name, but he didn't last very long, in fact we rehearsed with him but he didn't sing that day. He was some spotty herbert who didn't have a clue, and he used to shout 'Up! Up! Down! Down! Up! Up! Down! Down!', which had us in fits laughing, because was it up, or up up, or whatever. I played rhythm so to play the bass part I'd use the bottom four strings. Johnny wore some eye make-up, a bit of liner under his eyes, I didn't go that far. We played that gig, and then got drunk because we could sneak some cider, and that was really the point of the day for us.

We didn't play much more after that but we used to go to a club in Manchester, and drink tins of Breaker lager. It was a music club, so they didn't mind that we were fifteen, because we were A Band. We went to see other bands play. I saw Thin Lizzy at the Manchester Apollo, which was amazing. Before I went, my Gran said to me, 'You look up at that ceiling when you're there, your Grandfather plastered that.' I did look up, probably the only person in the place who's ever looked up at the ceiling during a gig, and yes, it was a beautiful piece of work. Watching Thin Lizzy was electrifying and that was all made by Phil Lynott, what a showman he was; the only bad bit for me was when he hung a United scarf on his mic. Oh, you shouldn't do that, I thought. I also went to see Rory Gallagher there. The electrics went out in the middle of the gig, and he got an acoustic guitar out and sat on the edge of the stage and played to 2,000 people. The place was silent as everyone listened.

Later that summer, my school group went for another week away, only this time it wasn't a religious one, it was an activity week – we would spend the time at Hollingworth Lake, a training base for the sea cadets. It was run by an ex-Navy man, who we learned very quickly we could wind-up by calling him General. 'I'm not a bloody General, I'm not in the bloody army, I'm a Commodore,' he would roar at us. And we did hate him – he made us run the whole way round the lake first thing every morning. The rest of the day we spent putting the sails up and down on boats before, on our last day, we were allowed to go out sailing on the lake. What a waste of time.

When I got home, though, all that was forgotten. I'd had a letter while I was away from the Manchester Youth Theatre; I'd applied to go to their summer school and I had a reply. *It's too late for an audition for you but come along anyway and we'll find something for you to do, maybe stage management.* Now this was more like it. I didn't want to spend the whole summer playing football in the field, girls were more interesting to me now – and here was an opportunity to spend weeks at a time with loads of them. I wouldn't have to write, I'd barely have to read. This was perfect.

There was another interest taking shape that summer, something that Mike and I would do together: drinking. The two of us had started experimenting by going to off-licences, buying booze to drink in the park, like most teenagers do, but we had a goal. We wanted to go into a pub, and order a beer. Two halves of mild, please – those were the magic words. It was a big thing to us, getting served in a pub, it was huge. By word of mouth on the teenage grapevine we knew there was a friendly pub, that if we went in there, we'd be served.

The day that Mike and I managed to get served in a pub was the first step down a long road for me.

Chapter two: the smell of the greasepaint

I found myself well and truly hooked by the Manchester Youth Theatre, which was run like a professional theatre. Geoffrey Sykes was the leader and founder, and every summer he would take a group of about three hundred children, and put on three productions. They would rehearse for three weeks, and then perform in proper theatres in Manchester: the Royal Exchange, the Forum and the Library.

I'd returned home from the sailing week on a Friday night, and then Mum took me down to a technical college in central Manchester, where the Youth Theatre was based for its 1977 summer stint. I quickly discovered that it was nothing like drama lessons at school – for a start, everybody who turned up was really excited to be there, they'd given up their holidays for this, so there was no-one sitting at the back of the room, moaning. There were kids who'd come from miles away to attend; some had come from Leeds and were living in halls of residence for the duration of the programme. Then of course it lasted all day, and not just an hour or two, but because it was exciting I had no problem concentrating. Although I did have to stop my morning paper round, as I didn't have the energy to do both. For the first three days, Geoffrey and his wife Hazel and their team ran workshops and warm-ups; and then they held auditions for the plays that we were all going to perform in.

When it came to auditioning for parts, there was a hierarchy, just like in any organisation. There were people who got the good parts every year, maybe others who were given okay parts, while the new kids – like me – would be expected to earn our way from 'Spearholder' to someone with a line or two. This was also true on the social side as well. Those who'd been there the longest were also at the top of the tree.

However I paid no attention to that. I auditioned for a part, and I was really cheeky all the way through. 'Look, if I stand a bit further back, when you throw things there's a better chance of you missing me.' I was just being myself – or at least myself as a performer – but this approach was unheard of. Normally first-timers like me would've been expected to wait and, as I said to my mum and dad that night, this was my first audition ever. But I was successful and I got a part.

The play was called *Agog and Agape*, written by John Retallack. It was a new play, about twins at a funfair. I was very excited; I had a part, even though it was one of those parts when you're on stage a lot but without many lines, and the play was going to be put on at the Library Theatre. There was even talk of it going on to a drama festival in Leicester. One of the other actors in the play was Steven Pinder, later to appear in *Brookside*, and he's remained a friend to this day.

I'll be honest, it was an awful play and I wasn't a whole lot better. I didn't yet know about the etiquette of theatre, and didn't understand what upstaging meant. My part meant I spent most of my time on stage under a truck, with just my legs sticking out. Occasionally I'd pop out and say a line. At one point, I had to go off stage, and bang something and then come back on again. I walked off, banged the prop and the audience laughed. I warmed to this immediately, so I came back on stage, took a bit of a run-up and went off, *bang-bang-bang*, which got another laugh. Meanwhile the poor bastards are trying to act on stage. I couldn't stop, I loved the sound of the audience laughing, so I returned to the stage, and took an even bigger run-up. Off I went, *bang-bang-bang*, by now the audience are in hysterics and the assistant stage manager had tears rolling down her face.

At that point the director came running back round,

grabbed me and said, 'Stop. Doing. That.' But I was hooked, because I could see what I could do to an audience and, more to the point, to a pretty Assistant Stage Manager in the corner. I did grow up in the weeks we rehearsed and performed at the MYT; the youth theatre taught me all the things I needed to be a professional actor like discipline, timekeeping, ambition, and – above all – a tremendous capacity for drinking and debauchery. Backstage, in quick change areas, girls just took their clothes off at the drop of a hat. I didn't have to go out with them for months, there was no pleading or begging involved… all I had to do was wait for a quick change in the performance and bingo, off it came.

I found a lot of these girls – women, I should say, as many of them were older than me – mesmerising. For a start they hadn't gone to my school, they weren't from Wythenshawe, some of them were from posh places and they spoke and behaved differently to any girl I'd met before. One of them was from Wilmslow, which was proper upmarket stuff for a boy like me. Without the theatre group I'd have been as far away from a girl like that as if I lived on the moon. Making girls like that smile, or laugh, became my greatest thrill.

When we'd finished, we were all going to head back to our ordinary lives, and the girl from Wilmslow said, 'Are you coming Friday, Kevin?' I didn't know what was on

Friday but if she was asking, I was going. I quickly found out that the Youth Theatre ran a Friday evening club every week, at Manchester Polytechnic. It wasn't just a drama group, we'd go to the pub, or we'd go and see a band if they sounded interesting. One night we all paid £1 each to see The Vibrators at a club called Rafters; punk rock had just started to hit the headlines and I wanted to see what the fuss was about. I wasn't very impressed and I slightly lost interest in music as a result. I really liked the social side to this life and the friends I made then, like Steven Pinder, Mark Aspinall (*Coronation Street*) Nick Conway (who was in *Bread*) became friends forever. I still saw all my friends from home and from school, but this was a new group for me to hang out with.

As I was keeping up my interest in theatre, a few people started to look after me and to teach me what they thought I ought to know. Phil Rose, who was to go on to play Friar Tuck opposite Michael Praed in *Robin of Sherwood*, told me all about theatre etiquette. You must never eat fish and chips in a theatre (the smell gets everywhere), what the calls are, the half, the quarter, the five. That sort of thing. You won't see these rules written down but I was like a sponge, taking it all in. That was the first time I heard of drama schools, and how important that was to go to a drama school. It was all about training.

The following summer, 1978, I jumped even higher

up the hierarchy and was given a big part, that of the Chamberlain *de la Trémouille*, in Bernard Shaw's *St Joan*. That meant I got to wield a huge sword when we appeared at the Library Theatre later that month. Backstage some of the older actors were talking of what they were going to do next, about what prospects there were for work in the theatre, and what they had to do to get those jobs. I never realised that it was possible to do this for a living. Imagine having this much fun, and being paid for it too. I was getting to be good at acting, or at least I thought I was. I didn't find it taxing, learning my lines was never a bother to me. I'd never heard of drama school before but once it was explained to me that you needed to get into drama school in order to get work, that became my next ambition. I loved the camaraderie, the tradition, the history, and the discipline. I loved the art. Also, part of me thought it would be just like the Youth Theatre – drinking, chasing girls, and showing off at night. That's what I thought it was – doing that as a job, getting real money? I was bright enough to know there was more to it than that, but still.

I was never one for self-analysing, and so I never really thought about why it was that I liked performing so much and why I was happier being on stage than anywhere else – even though I would have described myself as quite shy then. I came to the gradual realisation that I felt more comfortable performing than I did being me. If I think about it now, I can see what was going on. I wanted to keep part of me hidden away inside, the part I didn't think people would like, and the best way I could think of hiding this was to project something else altogether – being the joker, the prankster, the comedian. Jokes, I knew, made me likeable to girls – girls of my age always liked a boy who could make them laugh – and that gave me confidence.

What was it I was hiding? I didn't know then and I don't know now; maybe that was the problem, there was nothing, and I thought that maybe there should be something. That what I was hiding was nothing but fear itself. A lot of people in recovery describe their feelings in this way; the sensation that other people, those 'normal' people, seemed to have an innate understanding of themselves and how the world around them works. That they have been given The Book of Rules For Life, which all addicts are missing. This experience was heightened for me because I felt under scrutiny, sometimes real, sometimes imagined, and the pressure was more intense as a result. My interest in music had started to tail off at that time. It wasn't just that the punk bands had overtaken the kind of music I liked, it was because I'd sat in Johnny Marr's bedroom and watched someone really, *really* good playing guitar. I knew then that this guy was something special – the melodies he was playing were way beyond anything I could even *think* of doing. He was very focussed, but I knew I could never be that single-minded, there were too many things I wanted to do. I never wanted to shut myself away and practice, practice, practice to be that good. I would never have had the patience, because other things – football, girls, the theatre – would have called me away. Drinking, too, played a large part in my decisions. When we took *Agog and Agape* to Leicester for the drama festival, I found that life on the road, where we'd drink in the day and perform at night, was intoxicating. The camaraderie that came from being thrown together away from home made me feel like some sort of Shakespearean character, out of the era of rogues and vagabonds; it all seemed poetic and meaningful. I never lost that love of the road and returned to it later in life.

Meanwhile, there was a bit of uproar at school as, over the summer, we had become a girls' school, Cardinal Newman High School for Girls. Us boys in our last year sat at the back in assembly and every class, wearing tatty uniforms because we weren't going to pay for new ones now as we were leaving. Ahead of us were rows and rows of girls. As we were doing our exams that year, we had, most of us, lost interest in school anyway. I knew what was interesting to me and all I wanted to do was to get the qualifications that would get me in to drama school. I've never been much good at sit-down exams anyway so none of my teachers had very high expectations for me. The rest of my friends had things sorted out: Michael Galway's dad had arranged apprenticeships for him and some of the others, Mike Dunkley was going on to study because he wanted to go to university, and Simon was going to work on the parks for the local council.

I went to see the Careers Advisor, as this was supposed to help me decide what steps I should take next. Most schools' Careers Advisors in those days seemed to have stepped out of a black and white pre-war movie, that's how much in touch with things they were. The idea that anyone might make a living in the entertainment business was unheard of to them. Now, of course, people don't even bother to say they want to make a living in the profession, they just announce they want to be 'famous' and assume that all the other things needed to get on – talent, hard work, experience, a desire to succeed – are unimportant.

'So, Kevin, what do you want to do?' His tone was weary, he'd heard it all before.

'I want to be in the theatre, sir,' I answered.

His eyebrows rose up. 'Really? In the theatre?'

'Yes, I want to be an actor, sir.'

'An actor?' If he'd had a pipe – and he looked like he should have done – he'd have fiddled with it furiously. 'What makes you think you want to do that?'

I explained about the Youth Theatre that I'd done for the last two summers, and why I felt it was the best thing for me. He continued to stare at me in cold horror. Why hadn't I said something he'd understood, industry or something?

'Well. Well.' He started to pull out some books from the stacks on his shelves. 'Let's see, if you're going to do that then you'll need the right qualifications. Do you realise that you'll need to go to drama school?'

Yes, yes I had.

'And to get to drama school, you'll need your A Levels?'

My heart sank. I had hoped there was another way. I worried I was lazy, but I just didn't get exams. I'm not unintelligent, I used to read an awful lot, but when it came to exams I struggled. He, meanwhile, was consulting some lists in his books. 'You'll need five O Levels and two A Levels for drama school. Which college will you go to for your A Levels?'

That was it – two more years of studying. More exams. I signed up to go to South Wythenshawe Further Education College to do English, Drama and Art.

My parents were pleased that I was going to go on and do my A Levels but they never pressured me about it. My sister had worked hard and was now a radiographer at the John Radcliffe Hospital in Oxford. They thought it would help me in whatever sphere I chose to go into, to have those qualifications behind me. They weren't against me going to drama school – as a family we were too much into music for them to be opposed to anything in the entertainment world – but they thought something solid behind me would only help in later life. They'd always felt there was a real value to education, not just from seeing what it had done for my sister but also for my mum, who was now a senior figure within her field as a district nurse.

I never had much conflict with my parents, I can only remember ever having one big argument with my dad. It was about music, and the noise I was making. I must have been a real pain in the house as I liked to listen for the chords in a record, and then try and play them myself. If I couldn't hear the chord, I'd pick the needle up from the groove and replace it to hear those notes again. And again. And again. I would have to listen to it loudly to be sure I could pick up all the harmonies and other sounds, so my parents would have to listen to the same four bars, time and time again.

It wasn't that that set my dad off, though. It was my amp, the VOX AC30 that he'd helped me buy. He got fed up with the noise and insisted I play in the garage where the racket I made would bother him less. I said, 'No, I can't put it out there, it's a valve amp, it's damp in the garage, that'll destroy it.' We had a proper stand-up shouting match about it. That's the only time I've had a row with him.

On the last day of school, as was tradition, we all went to the pub. By now Mike Dunkley and I were hardened regulars; we'd long ago given up wearing long coats, and putting on wedding rings to look old enough to order our halves of mild. I was smoking by then, too, although my parents didn't know about that.

My time at college was great. Johnny Marr was also there, so I had friends with me from the moment I arrived, even though we'd stopped playing together (it would be decades later before I let slip I'd been in a band with Johnny and that was only when a record label asked if I had any previous experience. Their jaws dropped when I told them who I'd played with). I was very lucky because I had a fabulous teacher, Carole Moritz, who, as well as being brilliant, took an interest in me. She was very formative in the direction I took once I went on to drama school.

Carole was married to Charlie Moritz, an ex-youth theatre man. Together with Charlie, I was in a purely improvised and very funny piece called *Idle Hands*, which ended up in London at the Shaw Theatre. I carried on doing the bare minimum of work I needed to keep on with my three A Levels, while Carole and I worked on my audition speeches for drama school. She felt that I could go up for audition at the end of my first year, and I wasn't going to argue with her. With her help, I had chosen to do two pieces for my auditions: a speech by Mercutio from *Romeo and Juliet*, and one from a Mike Stott play called *Soldiers Talking, Cleanly* which had been on BBC's 'Play for Today' just before Christmas, 1978.

So at age seventeen I started auditioning for drama schools. I hadn't, at that time, even read *Romeo and Juliet*, but Carole had told me what it was about, so I knew what I had to say and do. I came down on the train to an audition in London, but that didn't go as well as I'd have liked it to, and I have to put this down to my own lack of experience, and naivety. I was at the Central School in Chalk Farm and I did my pieces, and then, after some umm-ing and ah-ing, one of the people on the panel watching me said, 'Yes, good. Thanks. Now, can you do the same speech, that last one, but do it as if you were a polar bear waiting at a bus stop?'

I thought he was mad. This was bullshit, as far as I was concerned, what was he talking about? I couldn't see what he was asking me to do had anything to do with acting on stage, it was just farcical. Then I thought, I bet he just wants to make a fool of me. He doesn't like me and wants me to look like a complete idiot standing here pretending to be a bear.

I didn't know, then, that what he was asking me to do was based on a theory very much in vogue at the time. I still think it's a load of rubbish, but I don't have a chip on my shoulder about it all these years later. Needless to say that audition didn't go well and I came back to Manchester feeling bad; this was the first time I'd ever felt bad about the theatre.

My next audition was in Cardiff, and Dad drove me

down there, which just goes to show how incredibly lucky I was to have such supportive parents. This one went off a bit better, I wasn't asked to do anything silly, but I still didn't get in.

Carole thought we should try closer to home, and suggested that I try applying to the Manchester Polytechnic School of Theatre. I laughed when she suggested it to me: 'You're kidding, right? You know who's been there?' It was, at the time, *the* place to go. Julie Walters, Steve Coogan, Jon Thomson, Bernard Hill and Amanda Burton are just a few of its well-known graduates. It was a notoriously difficult academy to get accepted into, with an average of one thousand people auditioning for less than forty places.

I went to the Polytechnic in Didsbury to do the audition, the same two pieces, and came back. A day or two later I got a letter. I'd done well, they liked me, could I come back again and take a written test. My heart sank. I moaned about this to Carole but decided to get a head start as well by going out and buying an idiot's guide to *Romeo and Juliet*. I went back to the college and did my best at the exam.

A week or so later another letter arrived, offering me a place on the following year's course. I was so excited and showed it immediately to Mum. 'Kevin, that's great, but what about your A Levels?' I hadn't even thought of that, but no matter. 'I won't need 'em now, will I, not now I've got in.'

As far as I was concerned, I'd done what I'd needed to do by going to the college. I'd got into drama school, so what more did I need from the place? I didn't know you could just get in if you were good enough. Imagine what that did to my ego. I knew nothing. I didn't even turn up for the exams.

It was the way I was, then. I'd become obsessive about something, be it music or drama, and then nothing was going to distract me. I was blinkered. If it didn't work out, there was nothing else going to happen to me, I had no back-up plan. I was lucky that I passed the audition to get into the drama school. This is what I want to do, that is what I want to be, that is what I want to learn. I had become driven to achieve what it was I wanted to do, and ignored things around me. There were obvious positives to this, look what it had brought me so far, but there were also downsides, as I realised over the next few years. I knew that I would drift away from friends, once I started obsessing about something that they didn't show an interest in. I regret this, of course; and over the next few years, despite the fact they were all so good to me, I started to drift away from my school friends. Of course I made friends at drama school but this was something I would repeat in life, making good friends but then not keeping up with them.

My school friends had looked after me once I was at college, and they carried on doing so now I was at drama school. I never had any money, as I'd spent all my grant money on buying a motorbike and so I did some bar work, on odd nights. When my mates said, 'C'mon, we're all going to the pub,' I'd say that I couldn't make it that evening. They would press me to join them, and once I got there they never asked me to pay for a round, but bought me drinks instead. They were mostly working and they knew I had very little, but I didn't repay them well; when I moved down to London, I stopped being in touch. I still regret that.

Drama school was something else, a real step-up in what I had to know about acting. There were only eighteen of us in our year group, the groups were very small. In my first term I suddenly entered the world of received pronunciation, and phonetics – what the feck was all this about, I didn't understand hardly any of it. I was the youngest in my year and still at that stage where I couldn't get out of bed in the morning. Those first terms were a challenge but brilliant, as we first-years weren't venturing out on stage, but attended classes in the day, and at night-time crewed for the third-years. This was a brilliant grounding in stage-management skills as well as respect for the craft and for other actors. It was a time when they wanted to equip actors with as many tools as they could to get work. The Poly wasn't a star school, it was an actor's school; we students were expected to go into the profession, and that was a very different story altogether from the sort of fun we had at the Youth Theatre. This was serious, right from the start.

There was always a third-year show on throughout the season, so we first-years were worked ridiculous hours; at our classes from nine in the morning to six in the evening, then crewing until ten, eleven at night. When one show finished we had to dismantle that set and build a new one.

It worked well because by the time we got to be third-years we were being crewed by the new intake, and that kept the camaraderie going that I enjoyed. It certainly helped when you were hanging off the edge of a flat at midnight, covered in dust and chalk and all sorts, knowing that the people on stage earlier that evening had all been through the process exactly like you. It knocked out any prima donna ideas of being a star of stage and screen, which I can only say was a good thing.

I wasn't the best student. I had moments that saved my bacon, where I'd do something spectacular on the acting side, but I was lucky that I didn't get thrown out. I knew what I wanted to do, which was comedy; I thought I had natural timing. I never imagined doing anything other than stage work, in the theatre, though; working on TV never even crossed my mind, there was too much going on. Mark Aspinall had just done a TV programme and he told me what it was like working on TV. 'Kev, it's unreal, everything's done for you. You get picked up, you get put in hotels. My mum came to the set and this girl was cleaning my feet because I'd been out in the mud, I was playing a soldier and I had to reshoot a scene with clean boots – Mum couldn't believe it.' We laughed about it but I didn't give it much thought. TV wasn't what I was learning to do here.

Drama school did me a favour, as the range of roles thrown at me did more to prepare me for the 'big outside world' than agonising and emoting over huge classical parts. By the time I graduated three years later, I'd played so many small and varying parts that I was ready for anything. My one complaint about the place was that over the three years I wasn't taken very seriously. Not that I really wanted the huge classical parts but I'd have liked just once to have been considered for a leading role.

However, I did get to play everything else: 'old bloke with moustache', 'young bloke with moustache', and even once, 'dog barking offstage' (no moustache on this occasion). I got to play a whole range of stuff. It was fun. They wanted me to play a dog on stage at one point – as a puppeteer – and I knew I'd hate that. But they also needed a bass player in the band so I picked up the bass instead; it was much more fun being a pirate playing bass in a pirate ship than walking round with a dog.

I also had a steady girlfriend, Sally, and when we both

graduated we left to go to Spain. Sally knew someone who could fix her up working in a bar in a little place – well, it was little back then – between Tarragona and Barcelona called Altafulla. I helped out as well, washing-up and playing guitar for the paying customers. I'd always liked Spain and the heat, especially after three hard-working years that I felt I'd spent indoors, in the dark. To spend the day with the sun on my shoulders was fantastic and for a couple of months we had a fabulous time.

Then one night I dreamt about theatres and lights and when I awoke, I felt I had to get back. I had to go home. I'd had this dream the night before, so I realised it must mean something. Sally and I got the bus back from Barcelona to London, which was hell; the only thing that made it bearable was the huge bottle of Spanish white plonk in a wicker basket that we had brought to drink throughout the journey. It was like electric soup. We arrived back in the UK, and I went straight to the drama school where I was told that someone had been looking for me. 'Who?' I asked. 'H. M. Tennents,' replied my tutor. 'Who?' I repeated. When he lifted his head despairingly from his hands, he told me that H. M. Tennents were the biggest theatrical producers in London. 'So you think I should call them back then?' He sent me flying out of the office in search of a phone.

H. M. Tennents must have seen me when they'd come

to our showcase, something that all drama schools put on for the final year students to introduce them to agents and producers. I was invited down to London.

I went to the address they'd given me, which turned out to be a theatre on Shaftesbury Avenue, and auditioned for a play called *Ducking Out* – a Mike Stott play, by coincidence – which was to star Warren Mitchell. I was trying out for the part as Warren's son. The audition went fine, thank you very much.

I had a chat with Mike Ockrent, the director (later on he found fame with *Me and My Girl*). It turned out they'd been looking for me all summer. He asked me if I had a full Equity card – at the time an absolute necessity if you want to work in the West End – and I said, 'No, not yet, I've got a provisional one.' There was a pause. 'Alright. We'll think about that, thank you very much for coming in.' I wondered what would happen next, and asked what they wanted me to do. 'Can you call the office this afternoon?'

I had no agent, I had no contact in London at all, apart from one friend; Brian Binns, who was then working at the Shaw Theatre. Brian was the kind of friend you could just pick up a conversation started two years ago; he and I went for a Chinese meal in Soho. After a while I said, 'I need to go and phone them, I've got a feeling.' I found a phone box and called the office: 'We're delighted to say you've got the part.' I immediately rang my dad, who was not in the least surprised that I had the job. I think he and Mum expected me to get every part I ever went up for. I went back to lunch with Brian and told him. 'Kevin, brilliant. You must come and live at my place now, you'll need somewhere in London.' When I went to the office to sign some papers, I gave them Brian's address in Greenwich, which turned out to be very handy indeed as the play was going to open at the Greenwich Theatre before transferring to the West End in time for Christmas, 1982.

There was one unpleasant task I had to perform. I had to go back to Manchester and tell Sally that we were no longer going to be living together, as had been our plan. She had nowhere to live, as our old digs had been demolished, so she moved in with Mum and Dad – never a great moment in any relationship.

I was in a different world. I was going to be appearing on stage in London's West End.

Chapter three: treading the boards

When I moved into Brian Binns' house in Royal Hill, Phil Rose, who I'd known from the Youth Theatre, was also living there. The place was awash with excellent pubs and the next few months became a mad period in my life, as the three of us hung out together, went to those pubs together, took the mickey out of each other relentlessly – we had a riotous time. I was rehearsing in the daytime and misbehaving at night, it was like school all over again but without any of the bits I hadn't liked. I never stopped to think how lucky I was – that I'd come out of drama school and found myself in work quickly, living with great friends – it just didn't occur to me that I'd fallen on my feet with such ease. I was just very proud to be in my first proper acting job.

And what a job it was. Working with Warren Mitchell was a revelation; I thought he was the funniest actor I'd ever come across. The play was a farce, and it kicked off my love affair with farce, because I was working with the Master as far as I was concerned. Warren knew exactly how farce worked and how to get a laugh in any situation. Bizarrely, we rehearsed in an old café in London Zoo as Warren didn't want to rehearse south of the river. Like all the cast, I'd been given a special pass but I'd arrive early and wander round and see all the animals before the public were allowed in. That seemed too good to be true and it was; in the end we had to finish our rehearsals in Wandsworth. After all those years of school and college, when I couldn't get out of bed and was late for everything, something had clicked, maybe it was because I was being paid but now I was always on time. It was something I took pride in from then on, being on time to start work every day.

I made my debut in November 1982 at the Greenwich Theatre, and Mum and Dad turned up. I was very surprised to see them there, Greenwich was not just a couple of hundred miles away from Manchester, it was a world away from home. I was now an actor, on stage, earning money. I was no longer a kid trying something out on stage. Just imagine how you'd feel if your mum and dad came to watch you on your first day in the office, or wherever you had your first job; that's how it felt to me.

Being with all these other actors, people with real experience and success in the business, was an eye-opener for me. One of the others in the cast was Kevin Lloyd, who later became well-known for playing DC 'Tosh' Lines in *The Bill*. We had become good friends, and in the bar after the first night he said to me, 'Kevin, have you got an agent?' I said, no, I hadn't. 'Right, come and meet Sara Randall.' He took me over to a circular booth by the wall and introduced Sara and the couple she was sitting with. One of them I recognised; the other I didn't. 'Kevin, this is Julie Walters' – I'd heard of her – 'and this is Jack Rosenthal.' Kevin sat down at one end, next to Julie, and I sat down at the other end, next to Sara. A few things were said about the play, and how it went, and then I tried to make small talk. I thought I was meant to talk business there and then, I didn't know that I was supposed to make an appointment to go and meet her at her office. Next thing though, I said, 'Are you going to be my agent then?' She looked a bit surprised but as everyone round the table started laughing I guess she can't have minded too much. 'Yes, I think so,' she said. I carried on, unable to stop myself: 'Can you get me work?' More laughter. 'Yes, I think so' she said, smiling.

I had such a great start so I thought I'd continue. I turned to the man sitting the other side of Sara. 'Have you been in the business long, Jack?' Everyone at the table now roared with laughter, but Jack was very polite, and said, 'A bit. I'm a writer.'

I blundered on. 'A writer? Have you written anything I'd know?'

He reeled off a list of his stuff. I tried to listen carefully but it all went so fast and when he said one title – *The Evacuees* – I grabbed at it, like a drowning man reaching out at anything to stop him sinking. 'Oh, oh that's my dad's favourite.'

It was about the worst thing I could have said. The others all began laughing again. I was rescued when someone in a leather jacket and carrying a motorbike helmet came up to the group. I know you, I thought: you're Indiana Jones's friend, Dr Marcus Brody. 'Well, I'm off,' the biker announced. Then he caught sight of me at the end of the booth. 'D'you want a lift, young man?' I must have looked a bit panic-stricken as Sara Randall came to my aid. 'Denholm, have you met Kevin Kennedy? Kevin, this is Denholm Elliott.' I managed to stutter out that, thanks, but no, I didn't need a lift as I only lived a few hundred yards away but it was very kind of him indeed. I wasn't really sure what he was asking – maybe he did only want to offer me a ride on his motorbike – who knows.

We stayed up late to wait for the early editions of the papers to arrive so we could read the reviews. Even if I'd dreamed of a perfect start to my career I'd never have thought it could be like this. The play was a great success, eventually ending up in the West End for the best part of a year. It was unbelievable. For a boy straight out of drama school, I was in work in the West End, getting about £250 a week, receiving decent reviews, and I even had a cartoon about me in *Punch*. I was told that people from Granada TV, the producers of *Coronation Street*, had been to see the play, because they kept tabs on anyone who was from Manchester and came through into theatre. They're always on the lookout to see who's good, especially if they're from the local area, and as far as they – or indeed anyone else – were concerned, I'd just about come from nowhere, as no-one had even heard of me.

Another one of the cast was Alan Devlin. It didn't take me long to realise – mostly because the rest of the cast told me on my first day – that Alan was from Black Rock in Dublin, and that he had to be watched all through rehearsals as he was a renowned alcoholic and if he had a drink that would be it, he'd be gone for days. He was as good as gold during rehearsals, though and didn't drink.

It wasn't quite the same once the show had been on for a while. One evening I arrived at the theatre only to see Devlin talking to people outside the front. Queues formed there to try and pick up returns and Devlin was walking up and down the queue, telling anyone who'd listen that he 'was feckin' deadly' and that they had to wait 'till the t'ird act, youse wait and see, I'm feckin' deadly.' He caught sight of me and declared he was off to the Lamb and Flag. I was pretty sure he hadn't been drinking as it was such a massive taboo to go anywhere near booze before curtain up, and I was still new enough to it all that I thought everyone would stick by that rule. He must be having a tomato juice in there, I thought. I should have known then what disasters the evening was going to bring.

I went in through the stage door, and asked one of the managers as I went past, 'What's up with Devlin?' 'Why, what's he doing?' came the reply. I explained what I'd seen outside. They turned pale. 'Where is he? What did you see?' 'He went off to the Lamb and Flag,' I said, and then I found myself propelled back out of the door. 'Go see if you can find him and bring him back.' I pointed out that I was due on shortly – Devlin didn't come on for ages but I was on in the first act, but it was no good: 'Well you've got half an hour, go see if you can find him.' But he wasn't in the pub so I returned and started preparing to go on. Someone else told me he'd shown up soon after, anyway, so that was fine. I went on stage as normal.

It was a full house as it was a Friday night, and as it was a very funny play we would have them rolling in the aisles. Towards the end of the show, Warren and I were on stage and Devlin was supposed to come on. He played a character living in the same block of flats as Warren who was a bit manic about supermarkets, and he was supposed to have a long diatribe about how to get round the supermarkets, saying something like, 'To cut down time, you go to the baked beans first, den you go to the cornflakes, den you go to t'milk, otherwise, if you go the wrong way, it takes longer.' By this point in the story, Warren's character had had a stroke, his face was taped down by make-up to make it look as if he couldn't move much of it, and the only word he could say was 'Porridge'. Devlin's cue passed and I started to flounder a bit when suddenly Devlin rushed on, stormed over to us, and suddenly stopped. None of this was what we'd rehearsed and, as I wasn't prepared for any diversion from the script, I didn't know what was going on, I hadn't got a clue what to do, and I was a bit scared. Devlin starts mumbling and I was so nervous that I had to sit on my hands to stop them shaking. Suddenly, Devlin walked to the front of the stage, looked out over the audience and announced loudly, 'Fuck this. I'm bored,' and walked straight off.

The audience laughed – they assumed it was all part of the show, I imagined, as it was quite anarchic, but I was liquid inside. I looked round at Warren to see what he would do, surely someone as experienced as him would know how to deal with a situation like this, he must have come up against people walking offstage mid-performance before, but I saw right away that Warren had a very wicked glint in his eye. He waited for the audience to focus on him and then he said, as clear as he could, 'Porridge.'

I said something – I can't remember what – and got myself off stage, where I found Renu Setna, who was playing the doctor, waiting for his cue. I dragged him on early as we were all over the place, but he wasn't ready for me and came on without his bag. He looked at me and I looked at him and then Warren repeated, 'Porridge'. The audience nearly lost it, and I nearly joined them.

By the end of the evening the whole company was on stage, trying to get the play back on track, although the audience didn't have a clue what was going on. Somehow we got through it and the curtain came down. That story has become legend, but not many people know I was on stage at the time, and I've been to places where people have started telling it, and I wait until they finish, and say, I was there.

Devlin was sacked, obviously, and I heard that he later went on and sang in *HMS Pinafore*, 'I am the very model of a Major General' and all that. He came on in his hat and the conductor nodded to the orchestra. They started up, *ompah-pah-pah-pah* and… nothing. He just stood there, swaying slightly, sword in hand, looking at the conductor looking at him. The conductor tried again… and again… and then Devlin walked off. After that he had a minder with him, it was the only way anyone would give him work, and the last time I saw him was a few years later when he came up to me in a pub, boasted that he'd given his minder the slip, and asked me to lend him a tenner.

I shared a dressing room with Kevin Lloyd and every

night he would strip to his underpants and shave in front of the mirror. I'd done my first bit and was on a high, so when I came offstage and into the dressing room I pulled his underpants down. I did it so often after that that he never even moved.

I really enjoyed being in the West End. Visiting the pubs and clubs after the show had finished, it was a playground for me. I'd start off in the Green Man & French Horn in St Martin's Lane with Kevin Lloyd. There are loads of actor's haunts in the Soho and Covent Garden areas, some of them have been there for centuries – and I drank in all of them. On Thursday nights I'd go to Heaven, the club underneath the arches by the river. I liked the flamboyance of the place. I became nocturnal. I was young, I had the energy to do it.

When the eight-week run in Greenwich came to an end, and the production was going to transfer to the Duke of York's, I realised that I couldn't easily live in Greenwich any more, as it was too far away to travel easily (this was in the days before the DLR or the Jubilee line extension that connected Greenwich to the tube network). Like many other West End shows, *Ducking Out* had a number of backers who ensured the show went on and hoped they'd recoup their investment. One was a guy called Bruce Hyman, who had a house in Kensington. Bruce kindly asked if I wanted to house-sit for him, as he was going to be away; well of course I did. A massive white Georgian house just off

High St Ken, why wouldn't I? Another amazing stroke of luck for me. In the end, the play lasted through the whole of that year, ending sometime around the winter of 1983.

Luckily, it's always easier to get work when you're in work, so while *Ducking Out* was still on I was asked to audition for my first TV play. It was another Mike Stott piece, called *The Last Company Car* directed by Stephen Frears who was well-known already for things he'd done on TV. He was about to make films like *My Beautiful Laundrette* and *The Grifters*. I thought him eccentric but a highly intelligent gentleman. I read for him and he waited quietly until I was done, then said, 'Yeah, okay, that's brilliant, have a look at this,' and he handed me a copy of *Spotlight*, the book for showcasing actors. 'I'm looking for northern actors, have a look through.' I thought, oh, I must have done really badly, he wants me to go through and find someone like me – only better. I plucked up the courage: 'Why am I doing this?' He looked surprised: 'Well, you've got the gig, I just wanted some help here.' What a relief. Northern actors, eh? I can do that. I went through and pulled out all the details on my mates, so Kevin Lloyd ended up in the film too. It also helped that, because it was TV we were working for, there was more money than in the theatre, and we were rehearsing in decent surroundings in Hammersmith.

Among the other backers for *Ducking Out* was a duo, Salzman and Broccoli, whose names you'll see on the credits as producers for all the early Bond movies. As a result of their involvement, I met Salzman's son, Steven, a larger-than-life twenty-year-old with great ideas and energy. He asked me to become involved in a project called 'Rock Over London', where he put recent chart hits on cassette tape with links between the songs, which he'd then send to radio stations all around the world. He wanted me to do some of the links with regional accents and he mentioned that if I helped him, I could stay at his place for free while rehearsing for *The Last Company Car*. This was great twice over. Staying with him meant I could claim, and keep, my expenses and also because he lived a much more glamorous life than me.

He said that we should discuss our arrangement over a meal so he booked lunch for the two of us at an Italian restaurant. Now, I'd been to restaurants before but only for a special occasion, birthdays or something like that, and never just for lunch. Afterwards we went back to his penthouse suite. 'Have you seen this, Kevin?' He held up what looked like a shiny album. I'd never seen a laser disc before – who had, this was 1983 after all – and over the next few nights we worked our way though his amazing range of films, all of them in crystal-clear quality. I did my recording work for him and settled into a routine of heading out to rehearse every day and then hanging out with – well, a playboy – every night.

One evening he said, 'I need to go and look at the designs for the logo, do you want to come with me?' Of course I did. So we got into his car and drove past the Royal Albert Hall, and then, shortly afterwards, turned into a road where there was a policeman waiting at a gate. 'We're expected,' he said, announcing our names to the policeman. We were waved through and I finally piped up: 'Where are we?' He had a mischievous grin: 'Oh, didn't I say? Kensington Palace,' and he parked and jumped out the car. I caught up and stayed as close as possible before someone realised just who they'd let in, it had to be a mistake. The door was opened before we'd even reached it and a man said, 'Follow me, gentlemen,' and led the way down a long corridor. 'If you'd like to wait in here.'

We found ourselves in a beautiful room, with a fire roaring away in the fireplace, full with pictures of the Royal Family. Not the sort of portraits you'd find hanging on the walls, these were family snaps, private pictures in frames on table-tops. I gulped. The door opened and in walked Lady Sarah Armstrong-Jones, the Queen's niece. We were introduced and I had a panicky moment of patriotic uncertainty. Do I bow? Kneel? Touch my forehead? I manoeuvred myself into something resembling all three as she showed Steven the design she'd made, a guitar with a Union Jack on flying through Big Ben.

I sat there very quietly, inwardly jumping when she

swore. Afterwards, Steven took me to Tramps, again without warning me where we were going, so I sat there in my combat jacket, jeans and trainers, drinking halves of lager because I didn't know what to do with myself.

The next day I walked into the rehearsal room in Hammersmith and said, 'You'll never guess what happened to me last night.' I told them all the details, but Stephen Frears just gave a knowing laugh.

To film the programme we moved up to Birmingham. I was put up in a hotel with the rest of the cast, along with Kevin Lloyd. When I finished filming my part, I went to thank Stephen Frears and say goodbye. Unexpectedly, he said, 'No, don't leave, have you an engagement? No? So stay, your hotel's booked, stay and watch and learn.' As I'd never had a hotel room of my own to stay in before, I was happy to hang about, watch the other actors at work, and see how a film was made. They filmed at night, and smashed a brand new Mercedes into the back of another car. To someone who'd never thought about acting other than on stage, it was all fascinating. I never felt like a spare part as Stephen Frears made sure I followed everything that was going on.

Fifteen years later I was on a plane to the US, when Stephen Frears walked past. I clocked him right away, but I didn't think he'd remember me from back then, when he stopped, and turned back to look at me. 'You're one of my actors, aren't you?' he said, which I thought was a brilliant line. I had a great comeback line too, as I was on my way to film in Nashville. I went back to Manchester to see Sally and to wait for another job. I was asked by Granada to go in and see them to discuss *Coronation Street*, but at the same time the opportunity to be in another play – *Keep on Running* – came up. I asked my agent to postpone the conversation with Granada and met up with the cast for the play, which included some of my old mates from Youth Theatre, among them, Nick Conway (who played Billy in *Bread*) and Mark Aspinall (in *Eastenders* and *Brookside*). It was a BBC play about a Manchester Grammer School in the 1960s. The play was to film in Cardiff so naturally we rehearsed in West London, in Acton – the Acton Hilton, as the BBC studios there were called. I had a blast, filming it in Cardiff. I played Pete, the school looney, I had very few lines but had to hang effigies of teachers all over the place.

I was going from Cardiff to Manchester over the weekends to my parents' house, to see Sally, who still lived there. Our relationship was at a low point. Sally was training to be a teacher and as the holidays were coming up, had decided to go abroad again. I hadn't exactly been faithful during my time in Birmingham, which meant things were looking bleak for the two of us. Filming had almost finished when Nick Conway fell seriously ill, and we had to reshoot a few scenes. I'd agreed to go and talk to Granada but now had to rush back to Cardiff. The producer's office rang: 'Look, it's urgent now, can you do it as soon as you finish – literally the day after.' We had a wrap party once all the filming was done, and I travelled back home to Manchester, nursing a fearful hangover on a Saturday morning. I went straight to the studio to do the audition and then headed home to my parents' house. I was going to head for bed and sleep for the rest of the day, or so I thought. Soon after I came in, the phone rang, it was the producer's office again. 'We really liked you in the audition, we'd like to offer you the part. The only trouble is we'd need you to start Monday. Can you come back down this afternoon to pick up your script?'

I got back on my motorbike, got up to Granada, picked up the script and then got to go home to bed. I didn't even think about what I was doing, really. The character I was to play was called Norman 'Curly' Watts, and he was only due to appear in *Coronation Street* for four episodes. They needed a brainy binman who could work out an accumulator bet on the horses so that another binman, Chalkie Whitely, could pay for his fare to Australia and leave the show. My first episode was to run on ITV on Monday 11 July 1983.

Chapter four: the street

'Morning Mrs Fairclough.'

This was my immortal opening line. Barbara Knox, as Rita Fairclough, was pinning up her washing. Morning, she replied. In case she didn't know, I told her – and the watching TV audience – who I was, and why she should remember me.

'Curly Watts. Used to do a paper round for you. Seven years, three months and six weeks since I left.'

Now this triggered Rita's memory as she recalled Curly used to be known as the Brain of Britain. She is rather surprised I didn't go on and do something with that brain.

'I did. I got three A Levels. See ya!'

And I was off, my first lines, my first scene, out of the way.

What could I do with just that short appearance on screen? I had no idea then what it might lead to but there were some things I knew I could do with my twenty-three seconds on screen. For a start I could think about the voice; he had to sound like someone who was bright, and I didn't want to give him a silly voice. I had no control over the character, of course, but if I put on a particular voice I'd have to repeat that again, and again – it would be tiring after just a few hours, never mind the weeks that I'd been hired for. I did fall into one mistake, though; maybe it was the way I appeared when I did my audition, but by arriving as the scruffiest bastard in the city, I ended up like that for most of the rest of my time there. The writers must have really liked that, having an actor who wasn't dressed up to the nines. I wasn't clued in, that's why, I thought it was like another job, I'd do my three or four weeks as this character, and then I could change my hair and become someone else for my next part. I had no idea it was going to be like this for the next twenty years.

To me it was just another job, best of all a job close to my parents so I could stay at home for a bit, which, after over a year in London, was a great thing for me. After all, I was a veteran of a West End show and a couple of TV productions. I wasn't someone who'd come straight out of drama school. Of course, that was how I felt until I walked into the Green Room.

The Green Room is where the actors gather between calls to work. They'll be in make-up and ready to go, but it might not be their scene rehearsing at that moment.

Coronation Street was the biggest thing on telly then, and had almost mythic status in Manchester, and I didn't realise until I walked in through the door, how iconic it was. Up to that point I hadn't watched *Coronation Street* very much – I was aware of it, of course, but what with being at college and then away working, I just hadn't been a regular viewer. But in the Green Room were all these legends, and I immediately knew who they all were. For a lot of people they probably thought they knew them better than their own families. Jean Alexander (Hilda Ogden), Barbara Knox (Rita Fairclough), Jack Howarth (Albert Tatlock), Julie Goodyear (Bet Lynch) and Patricia Phoenix (Elsie Tanner) were all sitting about, chatting. Now as a new actor on set they had no more idea than I did that I was going to become a regular like them. I might have been gone after a few weeks, for all they knew. But you wouldn't know it from the way they treated me. I was welcomed by all of them, none more so than Pat Phoenix.

The word 'star' is bandied about these days and, in my opinion, over-used. However, all of the people I've just mentioned were stars in the true sense of the word, and none more so, than the late, great Pat Phoenix. When she walked into a room you knew you were in the presence of someone very special. She was beautiful, intelligent and extremely fiery. What's the old line about James Bond – that all men wanted to be like him, and all women wanted him in their bed? Well turn that around and you've got Pat: men adored her, and women wanted to be like her.

For probably the third time in a matter of three years, I'd walked into something unbelievable.

After my first day I caught the bus back home. I had no car, I couldn't afford to run one, and I hadn't taken the bike to work. I sat down on the number 82 to Chorlton and thought, I've just been on the set of one of the most famous TV programmes in the world. I've walked on the Street. And here I am, on this bus going home, and nobody knows.

I did my first block of episodes, and the producers liked that, and asked if I could come back and do more in three weeks' time. Well I liked the role, and I liked the other actors, they were all good to me. I was also working with the elite, occupying the highest peak on British TV. That was a hell of an experience, walking into that. The money was good, as I didn't start on the bottom rung, because of my previous experience, plus I liked the perks, too, and life on set was very comfortable. What more could I want when I was in my early twenties? It was the easiest decision I ever made. I rented a flat, and Sally and her sister moved in with me.

I was very proud of being on the programme, especially now that they'd asked me back, and I told my Gran. I was accompanying her on the boat back to Ireland, and she was very excited. I said, 'You can't tell anyone, Gran, no-one must know yet, you'll have to keep it to yourself all weekend.' She agreed she would. I went to the bar to get us a couple of drinks and when I came back she'd told everyone sitting around her, all complete strangers, that her grandson was in *Coronation Street*. Most of them didn't believe her, I had to tell them that my appearance wouldn't be on screen for another three weeks.

I had less difficulty convincing the next person I spoke to. One of the curses of an actor's life is that you go through periods of employment followed by periods of unemployment. In those days it was possible to sign on, to cover the times when you weren't working. I took the bus to the DSS office in Gatley, where Mum and Dad were now living, and sat in the queue waiting to be seen by someone. When I reached the front of the line, I prepared myself to go through the rigmarole of answering questions and filling in forms. As an actor, I knew it was never easy as work came and went like the tide, which wasn't a box you could tick on their forms.

The lady interviewing me started up: when did you last work, when are you next working, that sort of thing. I explained the situation. 'I've just finished a contract and now I'm out of work.'

'Right,' she said, not paying any attention, really. 'What have you been working on?' The glamour of the West End and BBC's Play for Today had escaped her but I now had a new string to my bow. '*Coronation Street,*' I said.

'Oh!' Those magical words transformed everything. 'So... you're in *Coronation Street*? As what?' I had to qualify it, I explained that I'd just had a little part, but... then I realised that suddenly everything had sped up. 'When's that coming out then? About three weeks, you say? Really?' The forms that had been sat on the table between us had now moved over to her side, and she was getting busy with her pen, ticking boxes. 'Well, we'll just do this, and this, then this, don't you worry about that.' I hadn't had to do anything so far. 'Who are you playing?' I was a bit surprised and hesitantly asked, 'Don't you want my details and the usual things?' She shook her head. 'No, no, we can take care of all of that.' It was quite funny, really; all the routine I had always gone through when signing on during summer holidays and times like that had vanished. It was a lesson for me, and after that, until the show was screened, I was always careful about who I told. I wasn't embarrassed, but I didn't want people to think I was lying or showing off.

Finally, my episodes were aired. People who knew me rang up and said nice things; it was just the reaction I wanted. One Sunday morning, about a month or so after, I came out of my flat, feeling ever so slightly rough after the night before, and went to get a paper and some things for breakfast. I hadn't shaved, combed my hair or even washed my face, I was just going down to the corner shop, a morning like any other. There was some problem in the road ahead and a little traffic had backed up but I took no notice until I came out of the shop clutching my milk and paper.

A car horn went off. Then another. Some kids in one of the cars waved at me. Did I know them? Then the mum in the passenger seat wound her window down, pointing in my direction to her husband. I looked over my shoulder, what had she seen? I looked at a brick wall. I looked back at the car, and the cars waved even more excitedly. At me.

I couldn't help myself. I looked round again, it really was me they were waving at. I waved back unconvincingly, just in case they said, no, not you, and then carried on back to my flat. As soon as I started looking I realised quite a few other people in the traffic jam were looking my way and pointing. I hurried inside, put my things down on the table, rushed to the bathroom and furiously brushed my teeth, then showered and shaved. A bit late perhaps but I didn't know what else to do – that had never happened to me before, and I felt so scruffy. I was pleased, but slightly alarmed as well.

I had another experience soon after that where I realised I wasn't comfortable being in the public eye. I was asked to open a village fete in Gatley. I arrived on my motorbike just as I heard my name being called over the PA to come to the stage. I hadn't even got off my bike and I could see people moving to the stage, families and their kids. I panicked, I thought I couldn't handle that, so I stayed on my bike and drove off, without saying anything to anyone. I felt bad that I'd let people down but I had to learn how to handle public expectation. I told my mum, she said not to worry about it, that it was all going to take a bit of getting used to.

Luckily, as I got to know the other actors on *Coronation Street* I was given a lot of guidance on how to deal with situations like that, mostly by Geoffrey Hughes (Eddie Yeats). Of course I didn't ask for help – at that age you feel stupid asking, so I did what I always did – I watched, and learned. Geoff took me with him one evening when he was going to play in an Irish pub in Levenshulme; he loved his folk music and he played the Irish drum, the *bodhran*. He was brilliant at it and people would have flocked to speak to him whether he was on TV or not, he was that good. I watched him with the public; it was great how he dealt with them. He was himself, there was no edge to it, it was effortless; he was human and kind and showed an interest. He became the gauge of how I should do it.

The other big influence on me was Pat Phoenix. She was a woman with a brilliant mix of grandeur and the ability to make people feel at ease, wherever she was. I was lucky that she took me under her wing, and she taught me to be polite to people who came up to me. I was with the same agent as her, and it was probably that – along with my West End credit – which convinced her I was worth looking after. She was going out with Tony Booth at the time and she invited me to her engagement party. It was at a very posh gold club somewhere, I managed to get a suit to wear to the party but Dad had to drive me there as I had no way of getting to it otherwise. It was full of Manchester's socialites, and I bet I was the only one who'd been brought to the party by his parents.

The first scene I had where I had quite a big share of the script was at the Ogdens, with Jean Alexander (Hilda Ogden), and Geoff Hughes. Every time they went for a take, one that we'd rehearsed three or four times beforehand, Jean would say, 'Good luck everyone.' It frightened me. Why? What did we need luck for? I was surprised by how tense I became, knowing this was my first chance to be properly noticed on camera, and I asked Geoff Hughes why she kept doing it. 'It's just something that Jean says, God love her,' he said to me. He could see I was getting worked up in advance of my speech. 'Calm down, take your time, it'll be alright.' It was a light bulb moment for me. Once I'd done that, slowed down, there was no stopping me – I now knew the secret to speaking on TV: take your time.

The writing on that show was always superb, but that's no surprise when you look at the list of people who've worked on the scripts. There was nothing like us on television then.

The calibre of the people the producers could bring in, in all the areas of the show, was second to none. We gripped the nation, two times a week, every Monday and Wednesday – and I started to settle in. I enjoyed playing the underdog, and underplayed everything. The character soon became really liked because he wasn't the usual flamboyant cocky Northerner – he was a diffident, likeable character, and I was getting good notices. I got used to life on set, gradually. Working on TV can be long and boring. If you're not busy in front of the camera or rehearsing, then you're sitting around waiting. TV people aren't alone in this; it's true all the way across the entertainment world. One of the Rolling Stones was asked to sum up his twenty-five years in rock'n'roll, and the reply was: 'It's five years playing, twenty years hanging about.'When I first started on *Coronation Street* we put two shows out a week. On a Monday morning, we'd shoot anything that had to be filmed outside. That afternoon, all day Tuesday, and Wednesday mornings were rehearsal days. On Wednesday afternoons we went through what we called the producer's run, where we would go through both the episodes we'd been rehearsing in one go for the producers; any glitches, anything they didn't like, was picked up then. Then we spent Thursday and Friday filming the two episodes coming up, which could make for a long couple of days. We had the weekend off, which if you were going to be busy the following week, meant you had to learn your lines. It could be a long week if you had very little to do on set, as you were expected to be there in case things changed or the running order had to be shifted about at the last moment.

When the day's work was finished, we left through the Granada gates, where there might be a few autograph hunters, but that was about it. We weren't door-stepped by the newspapers the way they started to do later on; but when I joined, there had been a big storm with one of the regulars. Peter Adamson, who played Len Fairclough, was sacked for selling stories to the papers about the other cast members. It was the first time for most of them that this sort of thing – having stories sold about them by someone they'd known – had happened, and they all felt betrayed. The episode left a lasting impression on the cast of *Coronation Street*, seeing what the press could do to people. Now everyone in the Green Room was very wary around the press and became subdued when journalists from the papers were brought in by the press office for interviews. As a new boy, I immediately sided with my new friends and started hating the press too; you couldn't trust them, I was told, they'll get you drunk, they'll make you say things, they'll print something, even a rumour, and wait and see if you deny it. It was only later that I started to understand the game and made what I wanted out of the papers as much as they made something out of me.

It was thanks to my friendship with Pat Phoenix that I was invited to the *Coronation Street* Christmas party, a huge feature on the social calendar. I felt quite giddy and excited to be there, walking in wearing my smartest clothes. The younger actors like myself who were invited were very respectful and scared to death in case we said the wrong thing to someone very important. Once you'd been invited to that, we felt that we were on the inside, not just an extra or a bit part. But there was one problem; I was still only appearing to do a few shows at a time, I hadn't been put under contract and so I was only earning a basic wage, probably about £200 an episode. Most of the rest of the cast would be paid even if they weren't needed on screen – that way they would always be available for the writers to work with, depending on what storylines were running at the time, and whether they had to change them. (Sometimes the storylines needed to change because of something that happened to the actors – or something that happened in the real world.) I was only paid for the shows I did, which meant I was sitting about more than I wanted to, doing little and earning nothing. More to the point, I was easy to get rid of if it was decided I wasn't needed; I had no job security at all. It also meant I didn't want to spend money I didn't have, so I arrived at the biggest party of the Christmas season by bus.

That was why I was still on the look-out for other work.

I was cast in the farce, *No Sex Please, We're British*. I took over from Andrew Sachs, to do the northern leg of the play – the first time it'd been out of London. It was great to be back on stage, it was the first time I'd toured, and I loved that experience, it was something I'd come back to time and again. The feeling of getting on a coach, leaving a town behind, going somewhere new; it wasn't just a physical sensation for me, it was a mental one as well. What had happened in one place stayed there, and I could be someone new when we turned up in the next town.

I also enjoyed being back in live theatre again. Just before I walked on, I still had a bit of stage fright, but I found that energising rather than off-putting, now that I knew how to deal with it. And I was on stage all the time, doing my own stunts, such as jumping in and out of windows, tripping and falling over things, all of this getting laughs from the audience – it was great to hear an audience again after being on a TV set.

When I returned to Granada I found there had been sounds of displeasure about my absence, but as no-one said anything to me I carried on as before. After all, Pat Phoenix had done the play a couple of times, why couldn't I? I kept an eye on other opportunities and when someone said to me that *Hamlet* was being cast for a production in Sheffield, I thought I'd go for it. I was cast as one of the gravediggers, along with John Sessions. When I told

Granada about it there were a few shocked faces. They weren't alone. After staggering along for a few months longer than it needed, my relationship with Sally came to a sad and sorry end. I even thought we might get married, but I didn't try hard enough, and Sally said she didn't think there was a future in the relationship after all. I was very young – so was she – and maybe I took her for granted a bit. Still, I was as miserable as could be.

Rehearsals for *Hamlet* started in early 1984. Unfortunately I'd made the classic mistake and arranged to stay with Sally's parents just outside Sheffield. They were a lovely couple and couldn't have been kinder to me, but to be in a home that meant so much to her, and decorated with so many things that reminded me of her, was little short of torture. It was a stupid thing to do, when you've had a serious relationship ended, you don't immediately move in with your ex's parents. They were very nice and understanding and so it was with little difficulty I extracted myself from the house and moved instead to some digs in Sheffield, a room in a doctor's house. When I arrived for my first night there it was snowing and I couldn't figure out how to get the heating going in my room, so that first night was a lonely, cold and totally unhappy experience for me. I was heartbroken.

At least working on the play went well. John Sessions was very good company as my fellow gravedigger, but

Hamlet is pretty short of laughs and I didn't find the days much easier than the nights. I'd reverted to my West End days. I was drinking after the show, and sleeping it off during the day – both ways of avoiding dwelling on what was going on inside my mind. Sally came to see me one day, she was with Mike Galway's girlfriend as he'd finished with her and she needed to understand why. We all went out for coffee and sat there over the table talking it through. I was totally miserable but instead of begging Sally to take me back, for us to start again, to begin anew – I said nothing. I kept leaving the table to go to the Gents where I would weep uncontrollably. I would then sit back down as though nothing had happened. I don't know why I did that. I still don't.

To cheer myself up, I rang Mike Galway to tell him about a particularly filthy joke I'd heard in the Green Room. I'd barely got the words out of my mouth, when I stopped. He didn't sound right. 'Kevin… it's Ray.' We'd all been at school with Ray Kavanagh. 'He's dead. Drowned.' He could barely say anything else. *Hamlet* is dark and tragic, and had enough gravitas to help me in this situation. A comedy would probably have been quite difficult for me to get through then. Somehow going out on stage every night to 'dig' a grave for the drowned Ophelia was bloody perfect, it suited my mood.

I went home for Ray's funeral. All funerals are awful

but this had that extreme sadness when young men of the same age bury one of their own.

Although my break-up with Sally was difficult, she was very supportive to me and I'm glad that she now has her own family and successful life. I'm now able to think of our time together fondly. I moved out of the good doctor's home and found myself new digs at a boarding house run for actors. It was perfect. My room was warm and there weren't many rules, which at that stage was an ideal fit for my mental state. The play went well, and we ran for a few weeks. One evening, Johnny Marr was playing with his band – The Smiths were now very big news – at the local university, and I went over to see him after we'd finished, and to properly catch up. He was pleased to see me and we discussed what we were both doing, it was nice for me to be able to say I was on TV regularly and in *Hamlet* down the road.

When I returned to Manchester, and to Granada, I found that going back on the stage also helped my work on *Coronation Street*. Things I'd learned on stage that worked, which got a reaction from the audience, I started to include on the show. Little things I'd picked up to make scenes more interesting, such as playing with rulers; I'd put one on a desk and *twang*. It all helped to create Curly's personality.

I decided to do something about the contract situation. At the end of the working week, most of the actors would head to a bar called The Stables. In the bar I saw Mervyn Watson the producer, and I thought it was time to grasp the nettle. I went up to talk to him about it, I didn't want to have this conversation in the official world of the office but here he was in the bar. 'Mervyn, can I have a quick word? I'm struggling a bit here because I have to go and get jobs on stage. Even when I'm home I still have to get the bus here, because I can't afford to get taxis and things because I'm not under contract.' He put his hand up to stop me saying any more – I thought, oh dear, he's not happy with me. 'What? What's this? You're not under contract?' He looked genuinely surprised. 'Er, no, I'm not. I'm just on a block of episodes. I've just come back from one gap where I've been doing *Hamlet*, and if another job comes up, then I'll have to take it. However, if I knew there was a future… ' Something flashed across his face, and he looked at me differently. 'I've got it now,' he said. 'I understand completely. Leave it with me.'

The following day, there was a contract on my agent's desk. Somehow, everyone had assumed that I'd been sorted out but as it turns out, I'd been missed off the list instead. Now that I had a contract, I was on a retainer; it meant I worked exclusively on *Coronation Street*, but it also meant I could now make plans beyond just two or three weeks ahead. The first thing to do was to get out of my rented flat and buy a place.

I bought Geoff Hughes' old house. Geoff was a good pal and he even managed to sort me out with a 100 per cent mortgage, he was good at that sort of thing. And he did more, taking me under his wing and as I grew into my new settled life on the *Street* I spent more evenings with him, now that I was no longer with Sally, playing music in pubs. I spent more time in pubs now, even working behind the bar in some when I had nothing going on-set for a few weeks. Now that I was a more permanent feature of life there I found myself invited to places, openings, parties, hotels, and health clubs. My head was certainly tuned. The comforts of working on TV, the trappings of success, were much more rewarding than a cold room in a house in Sheffield. Why would I want to do that when I could do this? I was enjoying the work, I was constantly on a learning curve and I was working with actors as talented as Bryan Mosley, or Alf Roberts, or Bill Waddington, who was Percy Sugden, and Jill Summers, who played Phyllis Pearce.

Some of the older actors, like Bill and Jill, had both been in ENSA (Entertainments National Service Association) during the war and would tell us hilarious tales of those days during the hours we spent sitting about in the Green Room. Bill was once, back in his youth, headlining in Blackpool. He bought a pig, put a lead around its neck, and walked up and down the front. People came up to him and asked, what's that pig for then? Now that he had their attention he'd tell them his name and where he was appearing – it was the cheapest and cleverest form of advertising. Jill told us a story about one boarding house where she'd stayed when she'd been touring in the 1960s, where there was one sitting room for the TV folk, and another, much shabbier one, for the theatre actors. The two must not mix, instructed the landlady, sternly.

I carried on trying to introduce new things to Curly's character. Sometimes I'd be told they didn't want that; other times they'd shoot both ways and show them to the producers to see which one they preferred. A lot of the storylines were to do with Curly's love life, I think they thought the audiences wanted to see him being unlucky in love, and that only increased the opportunity for me to introduce small farcical elements to my performance. We were never told much about the storylines, where they were heading or even if we were going to be needed; the only time I was warned was when I wanted to book myself some holiday and I'd be told that they might need me that month. There were always whispers about what plot developments you might be in but I never wanted to ask what my character would do – or, worse, make suggestions – as I never wanted to jinx what I'd got.

One of my favourite storylines was when Curly went to live with Emily Bishop. Working with Eileen Derbyshire was a joy, she's a lovely woman and because we genuinely liked each other, the partnership worked really well. Eileen is not only a fine actress, but has a wicked sense of humour – in stark contrast to her alter ego, the ultra conservative Emily. There is a front room to Emily's house on set, which hasn't been seen by the viewers for many years. When asked about this mysterious room, Eileen used to develop a murderous twitch and say, 'That's where I keep Ernie', referring to her long dead husband, Ernest Bishop, who was shot dead in a botched robbery at the factory. There is a part of *Coronation Street* folklore referring to this incident; when any actor complained about their wages, they were told how Ernest Bishop complained to the bosses about his fee one Monday, and by the following Monday he was shot dead. We were always careful how we asked about money after that.

With Emily, the comedy was gentle and sedate, very much based on what we were saying. For my next 'home', at the Duckworths, it was pure slapstick – and that was just the rehearsals. Some of my happiest times were with Vera and Jack Duckworth because neither Liz Dawn nor Bill Tarmey bothered to properly learn their lines, or maybe they just couldn't, I don't know. What they did though was write crib notes to themselves everywhere, scattered over the set, behind teapots, under newspapers, on the back of cereal packets or whatever came to hand. The notes were hidden from the cameras but visible to us, or they would have been if I was looking out for them. Of course I wasn't, so anything I picked up produced a hiss and a shake of the head. 'Don't touch that. Don't pick that up. Don't lift that.' It was hilarious. I'd known Bill for years before I joined *Coronation Street*, as Mum and Dad had regularly taken me to see Bill in his band, Take Ten, at various pubs around Manchester.

After I'd been there some time, we moved on to three episodes a week, and we had a new building to rehearse in rather than the old stables we'd been using for years. After outdoor filming on Monday morning, we then rehearsed until we filmed on Thursday afternoons and Fridays. It was more intense than before, obviously. Most of the cast went to the pub for lunch on rehearsal days; it was a drinking culture back then, and I got used to these liquid lunches. I remained professional, and was always ready for work, but being in the pub started to be not just an escape for me but somewhere I was more often than not.

I was fairly objectionable in those days. I was still young but the fame, and the money, went to my head. *Coronation Street* was still the highest watched programme in the country and we were often in the magazines and newspapers so I was used to being recognised on the streets now. People would call out as they drove past – 'How's tricks, Curly?' – because one of the funny things about being in a programme like that is that people recognise you right away, but they only know your character's name, not yours. Your character was an important part of a lot of peoples' lives, they probably knew more about you than some of their own relatives, but it wasn't you they were interested in – and that's not an easy distinction to make when you're as young as I was. I defy any young man of twenty-three not to go a bit mad – and I did. I became obsessed with money and was always talking about it. At family parties, I'd start telling my relatives how much money I was earning. I thought it was perfectly acceptable. To a certain extent, it's what we talked about at work. I was very proud of myself; it was me being naive rather than bragging. It was important for me that people knew what I was doing, and for them to understand that I was worth this – that proper producers were paying me this amount of money because they thought I was good.

I don't know where this lack of self-worth came from. I didn't know that was what it was, either, that kind of understanding came later. I bragged to my family (no-one else, mind) about my income because I felt they needed to know how valued I was, and that what I was paid confirmed this. I was quite shy, and didn't like fuss and being the centre of attention unless I was performing. If someone gave me a compliment, I would say, oh no, you can't mean me. If someone said I was wearing a nice shirt, I'd reply straight away by saying I got it cheap. This is a ridiculous thing to say, but that was my protection, putting myself down all the time. I don't know where that came from. It was a defence; I knew I had a talent, but I was embarrassed by it. I wanted to stand out on the stage but I didn't want to stand out in life – I wanted the best of both worlds. I wanted to go to the pub, go to the football with my friends, normal people stuff, but also go to drama school. I liked the idea of being very good at what I did, but not bragging about it.

I felt anxious a lot of the time and started having panic attacks. I went to see various doctors, I thought it was because of the fame, but they didn't suggest that as a cause. I realised one night in the pub that I felt very safe in there; that people knew me, and didn't expect anything of me, and I think in the long term that probably did me a great deal of harm – that I felt safe in a pub. I used to go to football with the same crowd of people who were there in the pub, we'd hire a bus for away matches and it didn't help that the more established Curly became, the easier it was for me to do extraordinary things. When I went to games at Maine Road I was invited into the players' lounge, where real-live Manchester City players, who played for the club I adored, who wore that shirt – they came up to talk to me, to ask me questions. I even got to take a penalty once in a half-time shoot out. It was a dream come true.

It took me about two years to get a handle on it. I wasn't

the best-looking guy in the world and all of a sudden I had money and was famous and single. The rest is self-explanatory, and I took full advantage of it. I defy anyone not to. I didn't behave that way on set, I was too sensible to do that. And I never used it in public, either. I did notice some things were easier – if I went into a restaurant, I'd be offered a good table. I think it helped that Curly was a character people generally liked. Mike Baldwin, played by Johnny Briggs, was not liked, and he had a hard time out and about, although he dealt with it very well, telling people: 'It's not me, it's the way I'm written, I was told to do that. Do you think I'd really be like that?' And he'd smile at them in his charming way and any hostility would vanish.

Johnny was lots of fun, and a great storyteller. He had been in films before coming to *Coronation Street*, he always played the baddie in Norman Wisdom films. He was also in *633 Squadron*, which had been a favourite of mine when I was younger. Johnny gave me a terrific piece of advice. 'Take up golf,' he said. 'You can go all around the world with golf. And you get to meet some amazing people, too.' He was right; I've been invited to take part in many golf tournaments over the years, and have partnered some of my sporting heroes. One of the most amazing of them all was when I played golf with Gordon Banks. About a month later I was at home one Saturday morning when the phone rang. 'Kevin, it's Gordon here, Gordon

Banks. I'm going out to play a round this afternoon and I wondered if you wanted to join me?' I had to say no: 'I'm sorry, mate, but City are at home today.' He understood, it was football after all, but even as I put the phone down I couldn't believe what I was doing. One of the greatest goalkeepers in the world had just rung me up to ask if I wanted to play golf with him, and I'd said no.

With my working week now settled, I found I had time at the weekends to do more than just drink and go to football matches. I developed two interests, both stemming from my childhood; I found out more about my Irish past, and I started to play in a band.

Both my grandparents were Dublin born, and that was a vast influence on our upbringing, and in particular musically; I grew up listening to songs which to me at the time had no meaning, but when I listened to the words later on I realised they were rebel songs. The stories I'd heard when I was growing up – I knew one of my great-uncles had died, shot by the British, and that my grandfather had stolen a cake, but I knew no more than that – came back to me and I decided to find out more about them. I asked around the family to get the full rundown. My great-uncle Patrick was standing in a cinema queue in Talbot Street in Dublin on his eighteenth birthday when the auxiliaries drove up in a truck, picked him and another boy – unknown to him – and drove them away. It was said Patrick had the words to a rebel song in his pocket but no-one knows if this is true or not, or just something claimed by his murderers. He was found the next day, shot through the mouth. The other boy lived long enough to say they'd had buckets placed over their heads before they were shot.

My grandmother on the other side was a very young girl and she sneaked in with a friend to see the body at the wake. She told her mother about 'the poor boy' guarding the body, and of course it was that boy she then went on to marry.

My grandfather had run wild after the death of his father – his mother having died when he was only four. He'd formed a gang and they'd tattooed a gang number in ink on their wrists; they found a gun, and he used it to hold up a cake shop so they could steal the biggest cake they could see, a wedding cake.

I made many trips over to Dublin as I became more fascinated by my Irish background and spent a lot of my time, when I wasn't working on *Coronation Street*, finding out what I could about my family's past. Because the stories were told in music, and some of the songs were absolutely beautiful, I found it also rekindled my interest in music. (When I speak about the 'rebel' songs I knew and the stories of my grandparents' youth I have to point out quite strongly that what I heard about was the IRA of 1916, the trench coats and tommy-guns, not the bombers of the 1970s and 80s.)

One night I was in the Irish Club in Chorlton, where I lived, and a band, The Borderline, were playing. They didn't have a bass player, only Jimmy who doubled up on guitar and bass. I asked if I could get up with them. I really enjoyed the evening and wanted to do it again; I explained that I didn't want any money off them, I just wanted something to do of a weekend. After the band had had a meeting, they agreed, and I then found myself gigging at the weekend in an Irish showband. I did some backing vocals on the odd song, but otherwise kept in the background. What I loved about it was the camaraderie. Every Friday night I'd finish in the studio at about 7.30, and race home. The boys would arrive in their yellow van at about 8.30 and we'd set off to go and play somewhere. We all had matching suits, and we played a lot of the old Irish waltzes, foxtrots, and quicksteps and people danced. Not many had danced to my playing before so that was new to me.

Not only did it teach me how to play live because it was on the circuit, but it kept me safe; these four guys were men that I could trust with my life. I needed that sense of protection. While people were out taking drugs in nightclubs I was playing bass in a showband. It saved my life, I think I would have gone downhill quicker without it. I never cared for nightclubs, I could never hear anything I thought let alone anything anyone said, and before I was well-known I never had much luck in them anyway. And I never really enjoyed the music they played in those clubs, which is why when I heard The Borderline I thought it was right for me – before I even thought of playing with them.

We became very well-known on the circuit, in an era when Irish families wouldn't send their young daughters out to see live bands, but it was alright for them to see The Borderline. There's a big Irish community in Manchester, and we had plenty of work.

On the weekends when we weren't playing, I often went behind the bar to work as well. I enjoyed the life of the pub, things go on in there that I don't think you can get anywhere else. You could get advice about cars, women, marital troubles, football, the latest jokes, political views – all life is there, for me. I loved it, and I loved the fact you could come in, sit down, talk about your day or some other guy could talk about his day.

I carried on moving about in Weatherfield. After Jack and Vera's, Curly moved into the flat above Alf Roberts' shop, on the corner. I got caught out by a newspaper about this time; Granada had arranged for me to appear at a nightclub to promote the show, but, as it was a week in which I was written out, I saw no reason to be in rehearsing and decided to take some holiday instead. When I didn't show up at the nightclub, one of the papers tracked me down to Corfu where I was happily sunning myself. After a bracing interview in producer John Temple's office, I was fined a week's wages.

Being on set for days on end when we might not even be needed, meant that we inevitably played practical jokes on each other – to pass the time if nothing else. When I first started, Julie Goodyear told me a legendary story: some years before, the cast were rehearsing as usual in the 5th floor rehearsal room, when a window cleaner winched himself into view on his cradle. Someone – Julie never said who – decided to prompt a mass orgy between the cast. The window cleaner, eyes popping out, hastily winched himself back down again and reappeared with his disbelieving mates to see the stars sitting around, calmly drinking tea and browsing through the papers.

We'd do all sorts of things to each other. One of my favourites involved Geoffrey Hinsliff, who played Don Brennan, the long-suffering husband of Ivy Tisley. Most Wednesday afternoons there would be a Tech run, which involved the whole cast running through the episodes in order for the Technical crews, that is, wardrobe, lighting, cameras, props, and so on, to ensure everything was ready for filming. The cast would wait in the Green Room at the end when we would be given notes, cuts to scenes and general information from the director or producer. Geoff had a habit of falling fast asleep on one of the comfortable sofas and would be woken up in time for his notes.

On one occasion, Tech run finished at 4 o'clock. Geoff

as usual was fast asleep and dozed through his notes. Someone suggested we alter the clocks on the wall, setting them on to 6.30pm, and then hide. One of the assistant stage managers was then asked to wake Geoff up and point out the time to him. Meanwhile over thirty cast members huddled tightly together behind the sofas and chairs and giggled quietly as we all pressed together. Even some senior members were squashed in this time.

The ASM gently shook him awake: 'Why are you still here, Geoff?' Geoff finally came out of his kip and blinked before looking around at the empty room and catching sight of the clock. Immediately he clambered to his feet, swearing away at the ASM, 'I should have been playing golf an hour ago, bugger it, why'd they leave me to fall asleep,' only to scream when the room erupted with noise as we all sprang up from our hiding places, laughing at the hapless Geoff.

As Curly's character aged, it was clear there was something of a theme developing in the storylines I was given. The press spotted this too and later on they came up with a name for this: Curly's girlies. I was very lucky with all the actresses I've played against and some of the storylines were superb drama as well as great comedy.

Shirley Armitage, who was played by Lisa Lewis, was the girl who took Curly's virginity – a funny story in itself. She worked in Mike Baldwin's factory and Curly had left working on the bins in order to further his education. This was when Curly was living above Alf Roberts' shop. The night when Curly is set to sleep with Shirley for the first time was one of my favourite scenes; Curly was in The Rovers Return, drinking nervously, before he can go and consummate the relationship. Everyone in the pub knows the situation – that he's a virgin and is about to change that, but Curly being Curly talks about sex in a roundabout way, in this instance in sporting terms. 'I've not made a home run yet,' he explains to Bet as she plies him with whiskey for his first 'match', and, sensing his nervousness, wishes him luck.

Lisa is a stunning black girl and her relationship with Curly was only the second mixed-race one in *Coronation Street*'s long history. Together we had to deal with some hate mail and some backward-thinking comments from the public, but most people were extremely happy that Curly had found a girlfriend. Bill Podmore, the producer, said at the time, 'Several viewers were disgusted that I could have sanctioned such a relationship; none of them had the courage to sign their letters, which speaks volumes.' Even though Curly and Shirley went their separate ways I remained friends with Lisa, and went to her wedding – I still see her now.

Kimberley Taylor worked at Bettabuys and Curly was smitten with her from the moment he first saw her. This relationship was a slow burner, and the story developed over several months. I don't think it was planned this way but Suzanne Hall fell pregnant and so they had to write us both out of the show for a while. It was good at the start, with awkward, clumsy dialogue; it was a theatre of embarrassment and I felt very much at home in the way it was presented. Kimberley's parents were brilliantly cast, with John Jardine as dad and Marlene Sidaway as mum. John is legendary in the theatre in the North West – he has a wicked sense of humour and always had a glint in his eye, a very mischievous actor. Curly had somehow managed to get himself engaged to Kimberley without actually asking for her hand in marriage. The Taylors' living room scenes were brilliantly written, almost Pinteresque, with long meaningful pauses and idle chit-chat over cups of tea and Battenburg cake that was 'just on the right side of moist'.

My favourite line of the whole episode was when Curly later moaned to Reg of his plight: 'I never knew that when you agree to see a man's tomatoes it means you have to marry his daughter.'

I have to admit I didn't want Curly to marry Kimberley. I thought it would curtail the character's comedic output, it seemed to me to be a one-joke story – although it was a good joke. It couldn't go anywhere; it was great for a few scenes but I felt we were treading water, the whole relationship was wrong because it just didn't work. I thought the public would tire of this. I became boorish and pompous in my

Me, Mum and Dad in Seaton, Devon 1965

Me and my sister Cath on a
family holiday in Devon, 1963

An early school photo
at Saint Pauls, 1969

Playing the role of Hamlet at
Sheffield's Crucible Theatre, 1985

A school play at Saint Pauls Catholic High School, 1977

From back left: Ray Kavanah, Micheal Galway, Steve Dunn, Mike
Dunkley, Peter Hardman and me at Saint Pauls, 1976

The letter that changed everything, acceptance into
drama school, I was 17 years old

Me and Mark Aspinal,
Manchester Library Theatre

Publicity shot, Manchester 1985

An early shot of The Borderline.
From the left: Brendan Falkner,
middle on drums, Dave Mear, and
then a very young me.

No sex please we're British -
British Tour, 1987

Elvis' car,
Nashville
- the one
he didn't
like me
sitting in

Tootsies
Orchid Lounge,
Nashville
'gigging with a
local'

Me and Stan
in Nashville
'proper
cowboys'

Me and Emily Bishop 'Eileen Derbyshire'
on the *Street*, 1983

My favourite home in *Coronation
Street*, Bill Tarmey and Liz Dawn -
Jack and Vera's

Filming on the QE2 with
Barbara Knox 'Rita',
Roy Barraclough 'Alec',
Thelma Barlow 'Mavis'
and the beautiful
Sarah Lancashire 'Raquel'

Des Barnes, Raquel and me
'the love triangle'

Coronation Street does Paris.
From back left: Me, Steve
Arnold, John Savident, Sue
Nichols Tracy Shaw and
Angie Lonsdale

Liz Dawn, Ken Morley, Suzanne and me in one of the many
Bettabuys scenes

With Noel Gallagher at Wembly Stadium, 1998

On holiday in Ibiza
during 'Gay week'

The year I had two birthdays after crossing the International Date Line, me and Dad celebrating on the Air New Zealand plane

Me and Dad and a delightful waitress in Tahiti

St. Patrick's Day in
New York at the Waldorf,
1991

Bunch of
Thieves gig in
Manchester

Saw Doctors fan
magazine - me
gigging with the band
in Manchester

Saw Doctors again.
Unfortunately, due
to too much alcohol
at the time, I can't
remembered where or
when. Whoops...

Bunch of Thieves publicity picture - we were all pretty
drunk on this shoot, somewhere in Manchester

The best day of my life - our wedding in Sandals,
St Lucia, 1996

Sacked and pregnant but excited,
2004

Katy May Kennedy with her Great
Grandma and namesake,
May Kennedy, 2004

Revisiting the past with the whole family, 2013

Me and two of my acting
legends, Thelma Barlow and
Jean Alexander

Me and my mate,
Jamie Stoddard with the
FA Cup, 2011

Me and Ryan Thomas, who
I've known since he was
born, celebrating 50 years of
Coronation Street

Me with my gorgeous
bezzer, Denise Welch,
who is a fab, fun Aunty
Den Den to our kids

Dick Whittington, Nottingham Theatre Royal

Chitty Chitty Bang Bang, Palace
Theatre Manchester, Louie Healey
(Denise Welsh and Tim's boy), Tim
Healy, Katy May Kennedy and me
as the Child Catcher

Sleeping Beauty at the Lincoln
Theatre Royal, Katy May Kennedy,
me and Grace Kennedy

Darren Day, Brian May (legend), Brenda Edwards,
Roger Taylor (legend) and me, backstage at
We Will Rock You

10th Anniversary of WWRY singing with Brian May,
'The Show Must Go On', 2013

treatment of Suzanne, I behaved badly, like a spoilt brat, and I have since apologised to her. She was very gracious. But I did sigh with relief when the storyline came to an end. I loved the stuff with Kimberley's mum and dad, the awkwardness of meeting them, and the interplay that led to my engagement to their daughter.

Curly was not a ladies man, he was just the opposite really, but during this period he had more than his fair share of good fortune with the ladies, and it always seemed to start with a bottle of red wine – something that in real life I couldn't stand. Of course we weren't really drinking red wine, on set we used Vimto, but as I never drank red wine myself I always knew that when a bottle appeared on set for me it could only mean one thing: Curly was going to end up in bed with someone.

One of those who fell for the bottle of red wine was Angie Freeman, who became Curly's lodger. She was a forward-thinking, independent, strong woman, while Curly was his usual dithering put-upon self. The two together looked very promising. So the red wine was poured for Angie, the inevitable happened and the next morning she was horrified and swore Norman to secrecy. This began a period of will-she-won't-she fall for Norman's charms. Being Curly, of course it was more a matter of won't she, before that one came to an end.

It wasn't wine that allowed Curly to bed Maxine, played

by the beautiful Tracy Shaw, but drink played more than its fair share. This was one of my favourite Curly moments; I loved this story because it was short, funny and charming. Unlucky in love as ever, Curly decides he's going to travel the world, and on his last night in the Rovers (equipped with rucksack, tent and poles, pots and pans), has a last drink with his friends, including the lovely Maxine. They both end up getting drunk and, as she walks him home, she declares that what he's doing is so romantic that it has totally changed the way she thinks about him. When they arrive at his front door, Curly thinks he's going to order her a taxi but instead she pounces on him and they fall through the door in a passionate embrace. The last thing we see is the door closing as the pots and pans rattle.

Later the next day the Rovers is stunned as Curly enters, declaring he never realised just how much he had going for him here in Weatherfield. The hungover Maxine hides her face in her hands at this moment. Jack asks Curly just how far he got on his world tour before he realised all this, and Norman replied, 'Knutsford'. This was complete genius.

After she left *Coronation Street*, Tracy had her own much-publicised problems with drink and drugs. She is now in recovery and is very happy. It was a privilege to watch her progress and it's always a joy to see her and talk about our good fortune to have survived up to now.

A lady's man usually has a secret, and Maureen

Holdsworth was definitely Norman's secret. Sleeping with a woman who's undecided about marrying someone is one thing; when that someone is your best friend Reg, it's very bad news indeed. When I read in the script that Sherrie Hewson, who played Maureen, was going to turn up on Curly's doorstep to share a bottle of red wine, I knew what direction this was going to go.

Maureen arrived in a state, wanting reassurance that she was doing the right thing. Norman was of course his usual kind self but the signals were misread and, with the wine, the inevitable happened. Sherrie is a fabulous comic actress who has worked with a lot of great comics in her career; she is a perfect foil but has the ability to get her own laughs. She is also accident-prone and can be dangerous to work with. While filming the scene on the sofa when Maureen poured her heart out to the embarrassed Norman, there came a point where she lunged at him in what she thought was a passionate embrace but he thought of as more like a wrestling manoeuvre. The two of us had a couple of run-throughs during rehearsal, and all went well, however when it came to the take, Sherrie became more excited, caught up in the drama. As usual she leaped upon me, only this time she kneed me right in the groin. I somehow got through the rest of the scene and when it was over, Sherrie looked at me and said she was moved by my performance, as there were real tears in my eyes…

Chapter five: home – or far, far away

There was one woman Curly Watts was always associated with, and that's Raquel Wolstenhulme, played by Sarah Lancashire. Some of the greatest storylines I was involved in were with Sarah, culminating in our marriage – and then her leaving me.

In real life, I had already married and divorced Dawn by then. My first marriage was messy, ill-advised and damaging to both of us, and although at the time I didn't like to admit I was wrong, now that twenty-five years has gone by I can look back with a clarity that wasn't there before. I blamed Dawn for a lot of things for a very long time, but now I realise I had my part to play in this very sad affair.

It was in a late night drinking place, Hough End Hall, that I first saw this extremely attractive Spanish-looking girl. She told me her name was Dawn and she worked in a local pub, the Bowling Green. I saw to it that I met her everyday there and soon we were very much an item. I quickly became besotted with her, so after about a month Dawn moved into my house and I couldn't have been happier.

Dawn's friends then were a wild crowd, they liked to drink and take drugs and party well on into the next day. With a little bit of effort, I fitted right in. The life I was introduced to was volatile and fiery and I thought I could handle it, but the truth was I couldn't, because I remained completely insecure. Worse, I became affected by something I'd never known before – acute jealousy.

Dawn had a habit of disappearing with the gang for a few days and this drove me to despair. I simply couldn't handle it at all. These periods were frequent during our time together, and in hindsight I should have just done nothing, but I couldn't. I fretted and tried to find her, all the time becoming more angry and riddled with paranoia, which then led to me feeling pathetic.

I have to be honest and say that during these times I was hardly whiter than white. At the time I was playing with the band three or sometimes four nights a week, so not only was I away often, regularly staying away overnight, I was often tempted to do things I shouldn't myself, like the occasional one-night stand. I always found solace and comradeship with the lads, my band of brothers, as we all loved playing live music and drinking, and they often had relationship advice for me; admittedly this consisted of most things between 'Just leave her' to 'Have you thought about murder?' Hardly helpful stuff, really.

Our on-off relationship lasted for quite a while until one day Dawn told me she was going to leave me, and instead live with one of her friends. I was heartbroken because deep down I really loved her, but I had long suspected the two of them had something going on. I'd tried to dismiss my thoughts as just my paranoia but I thought I was entitled to feel that way, and that didn't help my state of mind. A short time passed, I probably spent most of it in the pub feeling sorry for myself and then one evening Dawn rang to tell me she had made a terrible mistake. This was music to my ears, as was her next sentence: 'Kevin, I've just found out I'm pregnant.'

I could be her knight in shining armour, riding to rescue my damsel in distress; I've always loved the dramatic side of life and this appealed to me greatly. I went to collect her and her belongings from the flat where she was staying and whisked her back to my house where we immediately started making plans for the baby. For a while, things were good between the two of us. Dawn's pregnancy meant that she became dependant on me, she wasn't partying with her friends, and we formed a cosy little home together. I thought the arrival of a baby would not only cure my paranoia but would change everything between us, all the problems we'd had would melt away. Like many before me, and no doubt many more to come, I was very, very wrong.

The next few months passed in a happy blur and on January 13th 1987, our son Ryan was born. I loved him from the moment he opened his eyes, and for a while all was well. Dawn was an excellent mother and handled her new responsibilities very well. I, on the other hand, did not. Fatherhood is an odd thing for a new dad. Until the baby has arrived, the dad's habits haven't really been curtailed. The lack of sleep, the constant demands of feeding and washing and all that goes with it, come as something of a surprise to him, unlike the mother whose body has ensured she's adjusted to a lot of that already. Whatever the reason, though, my bad habits – drinking, staying out – started up again. Seeing as Dawn was pretty much housebound, she became understandably resentful of my attitudes and behaviour.

Things over the next several months started to go from bad to worse. Loud and nasty fights became the norm. My paranoia was now back and at full volume, so guess what I decided the answer was? I decided we should get married.

I know. I know. I can hear you from here, dear reader, but then I was young, daft, and quite possibly clinically insane. Looking back it was never going to work, it was my last desperate throw of the dice to save a fatally flawed relationship. After a brief engagement, we were married that August in Manchester Registry Office, and then back to our local. Just the two of us, and that was that.

If that wasn't a bad enough decision I made an even worse one. I didn't tell my parents. They were on holiday, bought a newspaper, and saw the headline, 'Street's Loser in love weds'. They found out about their son's wedding by reading it in the next days fish'n'chip paper. They were horrified. Not that I'd got married, but that I'd done it without telling them, let alone inviting them to the wedding. Why didn't I tell them? I don't know why, even now. I am still ashamed to this day about what I did. I think it's because I was afraid of any sort of confrontation with them. I knew neither of us could handle that, because without having to have it spelled out for me I knew they wouldn't approve of my marriage. They had nothing against Dawn herself, it was just that they saw the whole relationship as a disaster, as families can, but, as people do, I ignored their feelings and went on to do what I wanted anyway.

Needless to say our marriage was not a success. I'd like to say I tried to make it work, but I probably didn't. I did what I thought I had to do for my wife and son, then spent the rest of the time – other than when I was at work – enjoying myself, either with the band or in the pub. I'd also become more interested in country music than ever, whether it was because of my miserable situation, or because we were starting to broaden the range of tunes we played on stage. I found it really spoke to me; perhaps because I was also learning more about my Irish background and connected the two things, in the same way that The Borderline mixed up the Irish and country music. We were playing old Hank Williams songs, things like 'There's A Tear In My Beer' or Merle Haggard's 'Tonight The Bottle Let Me Down'. These tunes seemed to mirror the feelings I had and, as people do when things aren't going that well for them, I leaned towards them. I loved the way the music from one culture could mean so much to someone in another. I also loved that I could play these tunes that were starting to mean so much to me, to crowds of people who also seemed to enjoy them; it made the moment so much more powerful for me.

When Ryan was about two-years-old I was asked by a magazine to travel abroad for a promotional piece for *Coronation Street*. Knowing about my love of music – and of country music in particular – they wanted to take me to Nashville. 'Cowboy Curly in Nashville', that sort of thing. Nowadays they'd make a TV programme about it but back then it was just for a couple of pages in a magazine. I don't think I asked Dawn, I probably just told her I was going, that I had to, 'for work'. I just wanted to get away from the cycle I was in, going to work, going to the pub, going back home. I wasn't happy and it was no-one's fault but my own, but I still wanted to get away. Of course I said yes, and then I asked if I could bring a friend. I had someone in mind.

I'd been to see a band performing in Yesterdays nightclub, in Alderley Edge, a magnet for footballers and expensively-dressed women. The band, Dougie James and the Soul Train, were well-known all over Manchester. Dougie James (his son, Ryan, is now in *Coronation Street*) played proper soul music, and they had a charismatic singer, Stan the Man. Stan was six foot tall, completely bald, and habitually wore bright yellow suits. He was a fascinating guy, and very funny. He had been around in music for a very long time, going right back to being in Hamburg when the Beatles were starting out there. I liked Stan's philosophy, which was very similar to mine, it's all about honesty in the music, if you've got fret noises on your recording it doesn't matter because that's real. When the opportunity came to go to Nashville I asked Stan if he wanted to come with me. He didn't need asking twice.

Stan and I went on the train down to London, and to a party his daughter, who lived down there, invited us to. I went round the party telling everyone I was going to Nashville the next day, because I thought it was the coolest thing on earth. The next day the four of us met at the airport, Stan, the journalist from the magazine, their photographer, and me. Now, I'd travelled with my parents before when I was younger, and I'd lived in Spain, but I'd never been on a jumbo jet before, I'd never travelled first class before and I'd never been to America before. I was more excited than I'd been in years. We flew on TWA and I had the largest seat I'd ever seen. (That was the flight that Stephen Frears wandered past me.)

We arrived at JFK airport and went through customs, but then were in transit there while we waited for our connecting flight. Stan and I went to the bar and I gawped at everything; everywhere I looked there was something exciting to see – yellow cabs out of the window, policemen walking past with guns (we never saw that back home in those days), and American people everywhere. Proper American people, not actors-in-a-film American people. At the bar I couldn't stop myself from exclaiming to the man sat there that everything was amazing, that I'd seen New York from the air, I was so overawed by it all. He bought me a beer to celebrate: 'Welcome to America,' he said, though he must have thought I was insane. 'Thanks! Thanks very much mate, I love it, I think it's brilliant.'

We arrived at the Holiday Inn, Briley Parkway, Nashville. I practised saying this for taxi drivers, 'Holiday Inn, please. Briley Parkway,' but in case I got so drunk that I couldn't actually say it I also slipped one of their cards in my pocket. The first thing we did, after having a beer or two, was to go down to Tootsie's Orchid Lounge, just behind the legendary Ryman Auditorium. Musicians like Hank Williams, George Jones and other Ryman Auditorium greats, never had any money so they'd hock their songs to

Tootsie. 'What's this? My Cheating Heart? I'll give you $12 for it,' she'd say. Later on they'd buy it back. There's a sign right by the entrance, 'All Firearms must be handed in at the door'. It was a proper honky tonk bar, complete with one of the best collections on a jukebox that I'd ever come across. The graffiti in the toilets was quite dark: *General Lee may have surrendered, but I didn't.* This was different from the sort of touristy place I'd expected, it was real. We had a chat with the bouncer, who had long hair, wore no shirt at all, with jeans and no shoes. 'My name's Jule, that's Mule without the M. You guys from England? You know the Queen?' We sat at the bar and talked to him for a bit, I loved the one-liners that he came out with. I felt a great affinity with the people from the south. I think that's a lot to do with my Irish heritage as well, there's great links between those two. And of course there's the cotton connection between the south and Manchester. (Many years later I went with Stan to see Johnny Cash, at the Apollo. Johnny Cash came on, 'I'm going to sing you a little song about cotton,' and a woman in the front row called up, 'You don't have to tell us about cotton round here Johnny.')

The next day we got up early to go out for breakfast at a proper American diner. 'What can we have?' Stan looked at the menu. 'Oh, you can have pancakes,' he said. 'Pancakes? I'll have pancakes. Look, grits!' I had no idea what grits were then but I wanted them. Stan put his menu down and looked at me. (This is my favourite Stan line, ever.) He said, 'Hey! Look at me and you, walking around in America without our mums and dads!' I laughed until tears came out of my eyes but he was right, I was like a young puppy, bouncing about, excited over everything I saw – 'Look! A real American fire hydrant! Check that out!'

We were there for a week, and crammed in as much as we could. We went to the Johnny Cash museum, where I was supposed to be photographed in one of Elvis' cars. The photographer arrived, and while he set up all his lights, the museum guide started telling me all about the car. I could tell he'd trotted this little speech out a few times: 'This is Elvis' car, he bought this in 1956, we have the cheque here you see, and this is his car, and this is a photograph of him with this vehicle. No-one's ever sat in this car and… ' Wow, alright, I'll be the first, then. As I slid down onto the seat, two of the photographer's lights exploded. I jumped up and hopped out of the car. 'I'm not sitting in there, Elvis doesn't want me to sit in there,' I said. In the end I had my photograph taken with me sat on the running board, it was the closest I dared to get.

Afterwards we toured all the famous Nashville spots, like the Grand Ole Opry and Ernest Tubb's famous record store. Stan knew a guy that was playing at the Bluebird Café, so we went to see him perform. We went to a cowboy store where they made stage clothes, and I was fitted out with a gaudy cowboy outfit, and had more photographs taken. I bought a dress to take back to Dawn.

The trip was fascinating, not just because of the places we visited but also the manner in which we did so. This was different to anything I'd ever known. Travelling first-class, having things arranged just for me when I arrived, this was an experience in itself. It wasn't so much about the privilege, it was also the way it allowed me to look about and see things differently, to speak to people differently. I felt my views broadened because I was not just a tourist to be fleeced, in the nicest possible way. I was a guest, and shown courtesy and hospitality I'd never known before. It made me think very differently about travel, and what I expected to get out of it.

I didn't drink a lot on that trip. First of all I was working during the day, I know it wasn't particularly hard work but I still had to be where the magazine people wanted me to be, on time and in good condition. But it was also because I was too happy to drink. I was only doing my heavy drinking back then when I was miserable and depressed. Stan and I were as good as gold.

One night the two of us went down to Tootsie's with the idea of playing there. The first night we'd just watched people get up to perform but we knew we had to get up there ourselves and play – it was an opportunity I couldn't miss. The stage was tiny but with only the two of us it was okay. Stan wore a bright yellow suit and, for some reason, a bowler hat. I was dressed in my mad cowboy stuff, and I played guitar while Stan sang. We did a couple of Hank Williams tunes, there's no better place in the world to do that, 'My Cheating Heart' was one. We threw in a Beatles number in as well. The people in the bar were incredibly generous, as Americans always are to anyone who performs, they're very supportive of people who get up and do things. 'Wa-hay! Yeah! Go!' However, at the end of our number, we saw movement from one of Jule's – that's Jule as in Mule, but without the M – fellow bouncers, as he leapt from the bar and punched a black guy clean through the door. He then grabbed the mic, and announced, 'Ladies and gentlemen, I didn't hit him because he was black. I hit him because he was a troublemaker.' Stan and I exchanged the briefest of glances and then played the next two numbers in a faster tempo than normal. Nevertheless, we had a great time, it was the highlight of the trip for me, and it wasn't even the reason we'd come there.

Before we left I took out of my pocket one of the promotional cards that Granada had printed up, the sort actors sign regularly, with my photo on it and space to sign my name. I wrote, *Came to Nashville, and did it*. The staff stuck it up behind the bar.

We left Tootsie's and took a cab back to our hotel –

'Holiday Inn, Briley Park, please,' I enunciated carefully, making Stan laugh. Then I spotted something out of the window – a policeman in the lane next to us. Nothing unusual in that, you'd have thought, except that he wasn't in a squad car but on a BMX bike. In full gear, with his pump-action shotgun, sidearm, nightstick, the works, pedalling along on a bike with a flashing blue light and siren whirring away. I thought I was going to die laughing, I could hardly breathe, and then our cabbie piped up: 'Yeah, I know, they look funny but they'll shoot you deader than hell.'

We found out later that the Nashville mayor had 'gone green'; he'd taken the police out of their cars and put them instead on BMX bikes.

As we sped along the road I saw a sign high up on the skyline. *Deja Vu – Fifty Beautiful Girls, and Three Ugly Ones.* I said, 'Stan, I know what we're doing tomorrow night now. We've got to go and see what that is.'

So the following night we had a drink in Tootsie's to loosen up and danced to some music from the jukebox, before we headed out to Deja Vu. Outside, once we'd shown our IDs to prove that we were both over twenty-one, we spoke to one of the bouncers to ask what the sign was all about, and what we might expect to see inside. 'Well, first off you need to know the rules of the house. The rules are: If you touch the girls, we'll shoot you. Bring your own booze in here, we will shoot you. We find you with drugs, we'll shoot you.'

I liked the place already and when we went inside I liked it even more. It was seedy-looking and all around the room there were big lifeguards' chairs with men sitting and watching us, wearing cowboy hats and clutching their guns across their laps. It was a strip joint, but this was Middle America, so it wasn't a den of iniquity, not at all, it was quite tame really. The girls had plasters covering their nipples, they weren't fully naked and all they did was just dance around. They were, though, all beautiful.

'Where's the three ugly ones?' I asked. 'Hang on, sir,' I was told. On one stage there were three poles that had been greased; and all the men started gathering around. At some point in the evening three quite big ladies came on, and all the men started putting money down. Stan spotted it before I did, it was gambling. They were betting to see which one could get to the top of the greasy pole first. Of course they took forever, because the grease always meant one of them, no matter how high she got, slid BANG back down again, flopping away as she did so. It was all a bit gross but funny at the same time. Before we left, I bought a t-shirt, which I treasured.

When I got home, I was fired up from the music Stan and I had heard – people I didn't know about like Lyle Lovett, Steve Earle and Nancy Griffith. I never got the chance to listen to the radio much at home, as I was up at 6.00am to go to work, so a lot of this new-style country music had passed me by. It's hard to describe the effect this music had on me; it was like hearing music for the first time, it was that powerful. I wanted to play music like this the moment I heard it. When I got back, that's what I started to do. I first had to get a band together to play some of the songs that I'd been listening to out there. I assembled a band from my friends and contacts. We rehearsed and then performed in my local pub. The gig went well so I felt we could do a few others. We played on a Children in Need telethon, and we even sang one of the songs in the Rovers.

Things with Dawn were no better after my trip. It was the first time I'd taken flight from my problems and I don't really like to admit this, as it's not a great thing to say, but I felt a lot better for it. I'd realised that my marriage was a massive mistake – I'm sure she knew it too. The whole thing was wrong, with a big flashing neon light spelling out WRONG across the whole thing. Mum and Dad knew it was wrong, I knew it was wrong, I'm sure Dawn knew it was wrong, everything was wrong about it. It was a disaster waiting to happen. But in those situations, who's going to make the first move? It wasn't going to be me. I was in denial. I was good at that.

I'd patched things up a bit with Mum and Dad but it wasn't properly handled, yet; I'd liken the situation between me and them to a pot on the stove, simmering away with the lid on. Everyone was being polite as it happens with these things because it's the thing to do. I did try and make an effort with my marriage; I invited Dawn along to meet people from work, but that never went particularly well. Dawn was shy in their company, or maybe she didn't want to be there. Once, we went to Dublin for a function and Dawn became very jealous and angry with me because I was talking to one of the younger actresses there. She thought my manner provocative. I suppose we were both prone to a little paranoia about each other's behaviour. It was inevitable – we were both too young, and we both wanted to be single. I was very immature and very controlling, which came from my insecurity at not feeling safe. About the only time I knew things were going well was when she came to one of The Borderline gigs; that was always a sign that we were getting on. But I wouldn't know for sure, because there was almost no communication between the two of us at all. She was quite happy with me not being around, she was doing what she wanted to do. The two of us just didn't work, but I didn't know what to do to fix it, and I didn't want to walk out because of Ryan. So I stayed, but I had realised that the only way to make this work for me was to travel.

I started getting panic attacks again, and this time the doctors put me on beta-blockers. I broke out in psoriasis, which was stress-related, but obviously the booze I was downing didn't help because alcohol dries you up even more.

I took to disappearing every now and again. Sometimes it'd be for no more than a night, perhaps to a friend's house, but I'd started reading books by the writer Leslie Thomas about running away – *The Loves and Journeys of Revolving Jones,* and *The Adventures of Goodnight and Loving* – and they struck a chord with me. I became a bit obsessed with the idea of flight. I started to see the idea of running away not just as an escape but a sort of romantic solution to my problem. I thought I wasn't just running away from something, but the act of flying off was itself an answer – that being away was the only way I could manage to cope. It doesn't take much effort to see that I was probably doing the same thing with my drinking.

I used to sit in the pub and drink, and wonder what I was going to do, how I was going to get out of it. Where I'd gone wrong. I'd get myself into such a state, I knew it was all my own doing, but I couldn't see an answer. As we approached Christmas 1989 I'd been hearing rumours about Dawn, from 'friends' in the pub; it got to the point where every time someone said they'd seen her out I'd put my pint down, drive home, confront her, be told there was nothing to worry about, get back in the car and go back and finish my pint. Then someone else would come in and tell me something else they'd seen her doing, and

I'd repeat the process. I was going a bit mad to be honest and when I got back to the pub after one such stupid dash I realised I'd had enough. I drove to Manchester airport and flew to Dublin, where I'd always felt spiritually at home anyway. I knew I had family up in Drogheda. This is one of those occasions where I've made use of the fact that I appear on TV. I got in a cab and asked him to take me to Drogheda, to any pub in the town centre. Once I was there, I started asking a few questions, and within an hour my uncle Brian Murphy – who I'd never met before – had come to collect me. Brian was just what I needed right then, he never asked me why I'd just turned up out of the blue like that, his attitude was, you're here, let's have a laugh, we'll have a good time. After a couple of days, Dad turned up. He too didn't give me a hard time, he didn't scold me, he understood. He didn't pressure me into talking about it, he just said, 'I'm here.' I never forgot that, that was a really close thing to do – you always think with your dad you're going to get into trouble, but he didn't. He never said a word other than, 'Let's go for a pint.' It was the perfect thing to say.

I'd later find out that what I'd done is called 'doing a geographical' – a recovery term; your mind thinks, I don't like it here, it's in this part of the world that's my problem, if I move over here it'll go away. I didn't know that at the time. I was in limbo on *Coronation Street* as the person I was romantically linked with in the show fell pregnant for real, and I was given twelve weeks off. Our story was put on hold. I was horrified. What would I do with myself? Of course what I should have done was go out and do a play or something – but all I could think of was to get to the pub and drink.

Luckily something else intervened. A few in the cast were approached to see if we would fly to New Zealand to take part in a Telethon there, an annual fundraising event that was popular there. I spoke to the bloke from New Zealand, who told me we'd be flown out first class and that I could bring someone with me to accompany me on the trip. Dawn didn't want to go – whether that's because she genuinely didn't want to go all the way to there, or she just wanted to get rid of me for a while, I don't know. I immediately knew who I should ask: my dad. We'd had a good time in Ireland when he'd come to find me, and I thought I'd like to spend some time with him. I'd realised that we could be away together, and I wanted to make it up to him for having let him and Mum down when I'd got married without telling them.

The Bloke From New Zealand rang me the following day. He asked, 'D'you know if Bryan Mosley would like to come?' I told him I'd ask Brian. 'Well, can you give him my number, so I can talk to him about what he might do for us while he's here, if he comes that is?'

What the poor man didn't know was that I played practical jokes on Bryan a lot, all sorts of daft stuff. I rang him and left a message on his answerphone, 'Bryan, you've got to ring This Bloke From New Zealand. He wants you to come out to the Telethon.' I gave Bryan the number and left it at that. The Bloke From New Zealand rang me again: 'Bryan's not rung me, mate.' I said I would sort it out and tried again. I'd barely got the first few words out of my mouth before he slammed the phone down on me. I had to call him back and persuade him that this time I was being serious, there really was a trip to New Zealand, and that this wasn't a wind-up. It took me ages to talk him round. When we all met up in the airport – Barbara Knox came too – he laughed at me: 'You, yer bastard, I thought you were having me at it.'

My dad had never flown first class, so I had great fun showing him what an experience it was. We had an absolute ball as the flight was a crazy one; as well as us, there was also Ernie Wise, some lads from *The Bill*, and, strangely, Kenneth Branagh, who sat on his own at the back. We flew out via LA where Ken got out, which he was probably relieved to do as none of us shut up the whole way over. From the moment we took our seats, Ernie Wise was cracking jokes, we sang songs, and of course we drank. I think there was even some dancing involved.

When we arrived at Los Angeles we had to get off the

plane for a while, but we couldn't leave the airport so we had nothing to do but go to the bar. I decided to impress my dad: 'They do it very differently here, you know, Dad. I'd better order. Watch this,' and I leaned over to the barman. 'Two beers please.'

My dad loved it, we were like two boys messing about, it was wonderful.

When we arrived in New Zealand – where *Coronation Street* was hugely popular at the time – we were given a proper Maori welcome. Being the senior cast member, Bryan had to receive the official welcome. If you've ever seen one of the Haka dances the Kiwi rugby players give before a match, you'll know what we faced; a huge Maori warrior threatening us, sticking out his tongue and waggling his spear in our faces, chanting and shouting as he did so. We'd been briefed a bit about this by someone who'd met us off the plane, but he was a bit laid back and I don't think he knew how ferocious this greeting was going to seem to some Brits. He also warned us that when the warrior came to the end of his greeting, he would place something on the ground, and that we had to pick it up. 'What happens if we don't pick it up,' I asked innocently. 'Well…' I could see this question had never troubled our man before. 'Well… then I guess it's on.' Quite what was on we never found out.

Our Maori danced and shook about, stamping his feet

and shaking his head. Bryan went up to his full height but I think that was more because he was trying to keep as far away as possible as he could, rather than because he wanted to stand upright. When the dance finished, the Maori placed a large shell on the floor in front of us. Bryan looked at me and I nodded toward it – I didn't want some major international incident to start by picking it up myself – so Bryan picked it up like it was a bomb, and I hissed at him, 'Bryan, you have to say something.' Bryan looked a little flustered; no-one had warned him he had to make a speech. 'Right. Er… we come in peace.' I collapsed to the floor laughing, but at least I wasn't alone.

Bryan told me on the way to the hotel that when he'd finished, the Maori warrior, this huge guy who'd just been threatening him with a spear, had given Bryan a big hug and a kiss and then whispered in his ear in a broad Kiwi accent, 'Love the show.'

We were treated like film stars at the hotel. Dad even had his own suite. As it was, despite all the luxury neither of us slept very well and, not knowing the time, we decided to head out, see what the place looked like, and maybe get a beer. Maybe we thought it was mid-morning, coming up to lunchtime, but once we were outside we realised it couldn't be that, as the place was deserted, and the sun only just coming up. In the distance I spotted someone walking about. 'Look, Dad, there's a local, let's go and ask him where we can get a beer.' As we walked up to the guy he caught sight of us and before I could even open my mouth he'd waved cheerily and called over himself, in the broadest Scouse accent: 'Alright there, Curly? What are you doing here?' We'd flown twelve thousand miles and encountered someone born about thirty miles from our home.

Later that day, Bryan bought me a present for helping to get him to New Zealand. 'Here,' he said, 'I bought you this.' It was a huge, whole salmon. He knew I hated fish and that I'd now have to lug this big dead bit of flesh with me everywhere; he was paying me back.

We had a great time in New Zealand doing the telethon. Everyone we met couldn't have been nicer to us, I had no idea until we arrived in the country just how big *Coronation Street* was then. One of the ideas for the show was for me to perform with a band, and the TV company had found me some guys to play with. I went over to meet them to rehearse; Dad and I bought a six-pack and drove round to the garage where they practiced, and we went through the songs we were going to do on the show. It turned out that they were performing at a gig that night and invited us along. It was a great gig but I made one mistake; I got up to perform the four tunes we'd practiced together, we did a couple more, some standards, and I had such a good time that I woke up the next morning with no voice.

After a slightly panicky day – I had to go on live TV

and sing that night – I managed to get my voice back, and performed as expected on the telethon. We had to dash about the place a bit, collecting money raised by groups all around the city; it was great fun.

While I was there, Dawn called. She said I sounded very happy where I was. I thought, I do, don't I? That was another sign for us both. It actually made it harder for me. I was still amazed by the reception we'd received, and now it made me feel like a fraud, because if I couldn't be successful in my own marriage what could I do? It just added to my sense of failure.

We had to return home but I really didn't want to go straight back. 'Dad, it's my birthday the day after the trip finishes. Let's not go straight home. Let's go to Tahiti.' He blinked: 'What?' I carried on, 'Let's go to Tahiti, we've got these round-the-world tickets, we can go anywhere, like Willy Wonka's magic tickets. We don't have to go straight back, we can stop.' He thought about it for a moment: 'Yeah, alright!'

So we flew to Papeete in Tahiti, where we stayed for a week. We were in a hotel that was made up of rooms in huts on stilts, overlooking the lagoon where the HMS Bounty came in. It was my birthday – twice – because we had crossed the international date line, which meant I had the excuse to get very drunk indeed. I was accompanied by an air hostess on her stopover, and the two of us went skinny-dipping at 4am in the bay. Where she sat on a stone fish. Somewhere in my head I remembered that I had to wee on the site, to kill the poison. So I explained this to a disbelieving air hostess and ended up stood there between these beautiful giant peaks on my birthday, peeing on this beautiful woman's bottom, with the moon beaming down. I was very tempted to sing, Happy Birthday to me, but good sense prevailed. The doctor we went to later on said I'd done the right thing, it was the heat in the urine that did for the fish's poison.

That night, Dad and I went into a bar full of French Foreign Legionnaires, who were being shipped out somewhere the next day so were making the most of the booze there. One of them was from Manchester, and he recognised me. So I joined him in drinking, until quite late in the evening, and when I could barely open my eyes any more, he gave me his kepi, which I put on... and the whole bar went completely quiet. Dad muttered, 'Take it off.' 'What,' I slurred. 'Take it off, now.' I persisted: 'What do you mean?' He growled at me, 'Take it off, now, and let's get out of here.' We scarpered quickly and it was only later I realised what would have happened if I had kept it on.

The air crew we'd met said to us, 'Don't fly home directly, stay with us in LA.' Well that was another offer we couldn't say no to, so we stopped over in Los Angeles as well. We went to one of the big malls and started pointing everything out to each other because we found it all so amazing. We looked like two complete hicks. Dad and I ended up in this cowboy restaurant for a meal. Chaps, it was called. A girl came to take our orders, she was very sweet and pretty, dressed up in cowboy-style, with chaps on, and her shirt tied off across her midriff. We ordered steaks, she said, 'Thank you very much,' turned round, and she had nothing on at the back, her bottom framed by the leather chaps. Once more we were made helpless with laughter.

I finally had to face reality and go home. My holiday away from my troubles came to an end. I realised as I walked up to my front door that I'd bought bits and pieces for Ryan, but nothing for Dawn; that just showed how little feeling there was between us both by then.

I went back to playing with the bands, The Borderline, and, more frequently then, The Bunch of Thieves. We'd started playing stuff on a different level to The Borderline, we were more of a heavy-drinking seven-piece shit-kicking country band. We weren't interested in recording, only in playing live – and drinking. I always found solace in music. A perfect place to hide in, playing the bass in the back. They were some of my happiest times. I used to love that big yellow transit van coming up on a Thursday night. A large part of that was escapism, but there was productiveness, there was something at the end of it. The tour bus became my new way of escaping all the things I didn't want to face in my life, and I was never happier than going to or coming back from a gig. We had songs like 'Pour Me Another One', and 'Little Town Hurt', all based around what I'd heard in Nashville.

The Bunch of Thieves were signed by a London-based agent and he wanted us to be more mean and dirty but I was very protective of Curly's image – he would ask, 'Can we make up something to put in the press about cocaine and drinking?' and I would adamantly reply, 'No!' I could see where they were coming from now, they were trying to give the band a mean image, but I wasn't having that; Curly Watts was too important to me. Drugs had never been much a part of my life, anyway. I was only really interested in drinking and drugs usually interfered with that. If the band went to festivals, drugs were often available, but you had to take them surreptitiously. I couldn't see the fun in hiding away somewhere when there was a perfectly good beer tent in front of me. I'd see people on drugs, maybe ecstasy or something like it, and they would just sit and stare at their beer for hours at end, as if it was talking to them. I'd rather drink it than have a conversation with it. The only drug that ever appealed to me was speed, an amphetamine that would allow me to drink some more. I only ever took it rarely, if I was too messed up on alcohol, then it would come into play, otherwise I wasn't that fussed.

Finally, things came to a head with Dawn. We were

leading entirely separate lives by now, and when we were in the same room together it was just row after row. We were both very volatile. We agreed to divide up our time so that Ryan was looked after. Saturday afternoon, if I wasn't at the match, I went to the pub until five, then I'd come home and Dawn could go out for the night. That was the deal and it suited me. I quite liked the pub on a Saturday afternoon, it's probably one of the best times you can go. I would babysit and she'd go out when it had been arranged. One afternoon I went out, had a good time, came back and there was a babysitter there who was furious. She said, 'You two best sort yourselves out.' I asked where Dawn was. Apparently she'd gone out. To me, that was beyond the pale, we had a deal and she'd broken it. The next day, I left for good. I'd tried to many times before but I'd never been sure where to go. This time, though, I knew deep down this was it. I packed a very small plastic bag, my guitar, and I walked out. I had a huge house and I just shut the door behind me and left it all behind. That was it, the end of a very tricky period for both of us. I got in the car and decided I'd ring my friend Ged, who played in The Borderline. Ged had recently divorced, and had room in his house. Over time his home would be nicknamed Heartbreak Hotel, because all the lads from the band at one stage ended up staying there.

'Ged,' I said, 'I've left Dawn. Can I come live with you?'

He said yes without any hesitation. I burst into tears, and cried all the way round to his house, every now and then I had to pull over and stop the car to try and get myself together. I'm not sure if that was self-pity, or relief.

I had to tell people – I didn't want to keep it to myself or to have people find out the wrong way, I'd made that mistake before – so when I arrived at work and walked into the Green Room, I announced to all the other cast members sat there: 'Hey! Guess what? I'm getting divorced!' There was a stunned silence. I thought that was the best way to make it real, to say it out loud, because then there was no coming back from it. I didn't really know how to express my feelings, as with everything else all I did was make a joke about it.

Nobody really saw me having problems because I was so brazen about it. People thought I was alright because I behaved as if I was. I wasn't of course, and one time Sally Whittaker, who played Sally Webster, caught me in the dressing room in tears. I used to have a lot of country music playing in the dressing room and it would always set me off. I think it was a release – I just had to get it out. She was very kind to me, she didn't say anything, she just came and gave me a hug. That was what I needed, but I didn't know how to ask.

Sally and I had always got along and that had caused some fun on one of the papers once. We went along to a fundraiser together and had our photographs taken, and then went home and thought nothing of it. The next day I had a call from the Press Department, asking what was all this about a 'torrid affair' I was having with Sally? It was just something made up to sell some papers and we knew nothing about it – that's one of the reasons why we were always cautious around journalists, because we knew we might end up being used by them.

That period in *Coronation Street* was about to become incredibly demanding. Ken Morley and I had started filming the 'Bettabuys' sequences. We had to shoot in a real supermarket so the only time it was available to us was when it was closed, on a Sunday. Some weekends we would get through thirty pages of dialogue (most of the other times in the show we'd have had no more than five or six pages). When Dawn and I split it was just at the very beginning so the pressure was just starting. Part of me loved it, as Ken and I had to be inventive on the spot. We were given quite a long leash to get away with stuff, that normally you never would – and I knew it wasn't going to last because this wasn't *Coronation Street*, this was something else. It almost became a 'Bettabuy' vehicle of its own, and that's not right, that's not what *Coronation Street*'s ever been about. I knew this wasn't going to last, we were riding the crest of this wave, and the writers were as well. How wrong I was. It lasted for five years. There were many different variations of the story with these two characters, and with the other people who came in – Maureen, for instance.

I stayed with Ged for a while. Brian Murphy, the cousin I'd found over in Ireland, called me up and asked if I could come over and do some PR for his firm. I persuaded Ged to come with me; he has a great memory for Irish songs and he was always very happy to travel over there to hear more music. We went and met my cousins' clients for his business and we moved all over the place before ending up in Dublin. The trip was successful for my cousin and we said goodbye at the airport, where we were waved into the VIP lounge – quite why I don't know as we looked more like two buskers, with our guitars, than anyone else in there.

In the lounge we were plied with drink, so much so that we almost fell on to the plane, we were absolutely blasted. When we arrived back in Manchester we were so slow, falling about the place, that by the time we reached customs the hall had completely emptied out. It was inevitable that we would be stopped: 'Where have you two been?' I slurred, trying to keep all the words in the right order, 'We've been in the VIP lounge at Dublin airport.' The Customs officer glared at us. 'And what makes you think you're VIPs?' If there was anything that was going to sober me up quickly, that was it. I knew we were in trouble. I willed Ged not to reply and he didn't, so he must have felt the same as me. We waited for the next question. 'Now, when you were in Dublin, did you come into any contact with drugs at all?' Ged leaned over, conspiratorially, and the man looked hopeful. Ged said, 'We looked, and we looked, and we couldn't find anything!'

We were whisked aside, everything emptied out of our bags, and then strip-searched. It was awful, but worth it for the great line from Ged.

Then one day I had a call from Dawn. I knew that by now she had a boyfriend. She asked to meet me in a pub, funnily enough one I'd walked into once with Ged and then walked out of straight away as it was awful. As soon as I arrived and said hello, she burst into tears. 'What's the matter, what's going on?' I was worried, was something up with Ryan? No, it turned out that she'd spoken about me to one of the newspapers. It was good of her to warn me, I suppose.

I decided I didn't want to be around when the paper came out and so I thought I'd go away for a few days. As it was early in March 1991, and I had a window of holiday coming up, I decided I would fly to New York for St Patrick's Day. I would need some company, though, and who better to ask than Dad. I rang him at work and said, 'What you doing next week?' He wanted to know why. 'Can you get a week off?' He ummed and aahed a bit. 'Get a week off, swap if you can. We're going to New York, for St Patrick's Day. Just ring me back if you can get the time off.' I explained that a story was going to come out about me and that I wanted to be away when it did. He understood and in no time at all he rang me back to say he could do it.

We booked to fly Aer Lingus and stay at the Waldorf Astoria for a week. It had all the makings of a great trip until we boarded the plane, which was full to the brim with noisy schoolchildren, heading over to take part in the parade. I knew that neither of us would be able to stand eight hours of this so when the plane landed at Shannon, where we went through US Customs, I played a card I had never used before – the fame card. I asked the staff at the desk to upgrade us. They were only too delighted to help and so we were bumped up to First Class. As we sat down I heard this voice looming behind me. 'My name's Paul Claffey, from WMIR radio,' and he proffered a card into my hand. 'I'm doing a live broadcast from New York City on St Patrick's Day, would you like to be on the show?' Of course I was delighted to be asked. He was pleased and said, 'I tell you what I'll do – we've got invites to every single St Patrick's lunch going, from Aer Lingus to the Bank of Ireland. You and your dad must come with us to all of these feasts.' He had with him someone he introduced as Johnny the Copper, from somewhere I never caught the name of. He was a guard, and he claimed he'd just gone out from home to buy a pint of milk when he'd bumped into Claffey, and now found himself on this plane. He sat there in a constant air of happy bewilderment. Every now and again, he'd pipe up, 'I think I'll have a wee tincture.'

Paul Claffey was as good as his word and took us everywhere, including to the Irish Embassy, where I met loads of senators. We had a fabulous few days and on the Sunday, Dad went out and got the paper. I didn't even read it. I asked how bad it was, he told me not to worry about it. So I didn't. To this day I still don't know what was in it.

I had a great time in New York with my dad. We were still like little boys seeing something for the first time. Look – a yellow cab! Look – a fire hydrant! Wow – the Empire State! We also went to see a few bands, The Commitments, which we both liked very much, and The Wolftones, which Dad hated because he thought they were anti-Brit. We went to a country bar and drank Bourbon all morning. We went and did the radio show with Paul Claffey; I bumped into Johnny the guard again outside the studio. 'What do you think John? How are you liking New York?' 'Fine fine, thank you very much. It's raining outside now, so I thought I'd come in and have a wee tincture.'

We had such a good time that it became a tradition for me and Dad to go to New York for St Patrick's Day. On one visit, a couple of years later, we were staying in a hotel and there was a rumour that Gregory Peck was also staying in the hotel. Dad had gone upstairs to get some money to change into dollars, and as he stepped into the lift on his way down who should he see but Mr and Mrs Gregory Peck. Dad greeted them politely. Now Dad loved Gregory Peck, but instead of asking him a pertinent question like, do you think To Kill A Mockingbird advanced the cause of civil rights in America? What was it like working with David Niven? And was it a real whale? Dad said, 'Alright Greg. Now, my son's in the business, too.' Gregory Peck blurted out, 'Really?' Dad filled him in: 'Oh yes, *Coronation Street*, you know.' Gregory Peck said, 'Oh yes, I've heard of that.' The lift came to a halt, and Dad stepped out. 'Well, lovely to meet you Greg,' and that was that.When I got home I was asked if I wanted to 'put my side of the story' by the papers, but I declined as I didn't know what the story was anyway, and I didn't want to be drawn into anything undignified. I've always had a good relationship with the papers and although I was always wary of them it ended up standing me in good stead not to have been drawn into a battle.

The bands came to an end, for me anyway, as I found myself working harder and harder at the Bettabuys supermarket. I had fallen back into love with acting. I wanted to have another go, try something different with that. I was very lucky, more stories were coming my way, more juicy stuff for me to get my teeth into. Besides, my need to escape my daily life had grown less. Ged and I continued living at Heartbreak Hotel, we were both single, it was quite a nice time. There was nothing wild and untoward going on, we'd both had enough if it by then – the last thing we wanted was anything serious. There were moments of complete and utter despair and sadness, when I'd go and listen to some country music and get it out my system. Or sometimes I'd play with Ged, 'I Guess It Doesn't Matter Any More' by Buddy Holly became a favourite.

There were people around me who were able to observe and deduce there was more going on inside than I let on. That I was carrying around a lot of guilt, among other things, for instance. Helen Worth, who played Gail Tilsley, came up to me in the Green Room when no-one else was around and invited me to spend Christmas with her and her family. Gestures of kindness like that were amazing but I didn't let on how much they meant to me, as although inside I felt very lonely I didn't admit it, because I didn't know how.

I decided to move out of Ged's house and buy myself a flat. As I was hanging round Didsbury a lot, where people like Stan lived, I thought I'd look around there. I agreed to give Dawn the house – all I wanted was enough to put a deposit on the flat – and after some time I was officially divorced, on account of my Unreasonable Behaviour. Ged was divorced for the same thing so for a while we called ourselves the Unreasonable Behaviour Brothers.

When the divorce was finalised – I don't remember the date as I threw all the paperwork away – I decided I would like to be out of the country, so together with Stan we thought we'd go to Majorca to get some sun. At the airport, Stan was his usual inconspicuous self: six foot tall, bald, in his bright yellow suit. I never knew when we were together if people were looking because there was Kevin Kennedy or were they wondering who this bloke was in the yellow. We walked up the steps onto the plane. Row after row of leather-clad Freddie Mercury look-a-likes stared back at us. I looked at the stewardess. 'Er... are we on the right flight?' She smiled. 'Didn't you know? It's Gay Week at the resort you're going to.' Her smile grew broader as Stan and I looked at each other. I'd booked the holiday. 'I swear I didn't know, Stan.'

Of course we had a brilliant week. Everyone we spoke to thought it was very funny, that we'd turned up not knowing it was Gay Week. I met a stunning German girl – who ended up selling a story about me, even though what she claimed happened never did – but that wasn't the only interest the papers had in me that week. When I arrived at the hotel I saw photographers on the roof of the hotel and I assumed they were taking pictures of me because they thought I was secretly gay. I didn't realise that they were stalking Keith Harris, the ventriloquist, who was staying at a different hotel in the area (I don't know why they were after him). When we flew home, Keith was on the same plane and he thanked me for taking the heat from the photographers for him – and the only story the papers got about me was a false one from this lovely-looking woman. We had had the best holiday for ages.

I know this chapter reads as if I spent my entire time on holiday, but that wasn't the case. I worked hard, and I felt I was entitled to a holiday as a result. But what I didn't know then, didn't learn until I was in recovery, is that I wasn't on holiday – I was running away. I was escaping my problems, or so I thought, and giving myself an excuse to drink even more. Who doesn't let their hair down a bit on holiday? The only difference then was that I was starting to drink like that all the time.

Chapter six: Bettabuys

'Right, now to business. Your badge of office. I now proclaim you Mr Norman Watts, assistant manager trainee.' – Reg Holdsworth's first words to me, as we started a five-year period of filming at Bettabuys, *Coronation Street*'s supermarket (now Freshco's).

When Ken Morley arrived on *Coronation Street* as Curly's boss and mentor, it began a whole new change of direction for my character. *Coronation Street* is all about double acts such as Stan and Hilda Ogden, or Jack and Vera Duckworth; but this was something new. For a start it was based around our place of work, rather than the street or the pub or the home, which was a change, not just for the audience but also us actors, as we had to film in a real supermarket, rather than on a set. This meant that for five years, from the end of the eighties to the mid-nineties, I was working every Sunday, trying to cram into one day's shooting a whole week's worth of material. It wasn't supposed to go that way, initially, but Ken is a very clever actor and a funny man, both on and off screen. The two of us got on famously and we put a lot more into the shooting – exchanging weird looks, playing with our glasses, funny handshakes, a lot of 'business', which really took off, so much so that the writers really enjoyed writing for these scenes.

Norman and Reg were two deluded blokes who thought that this outpost of the Bettabuy empire was the pinnacle of the organisation, but it wasn't, it was a far-flung outpost where they put the dregs of society. It had a believability that the writers immediately latched onto, people knew people like that. No way am I lumping myself in the same class as Laurel and Hardy or Albert and Costello but it had the classic comic set-up of the fat one and the thin one, and both of them bloomin' idiots.

Inevitably our workload on the show increased. At its peak, I'd be doing four episodes on a Sunday; that is, readying all our scenes with a technical run-through and then shooting all those scenes, for all those episodes, in that day. During the week, I might have a couple of Rovers scenes to film. Normally I'd have Monday off, and then I'd be in the studio with the other cast members so that we could rehearse during the Tuesday and Wednesday for filming on the Thursday. I might have no more than four lines in the Rovers but I still had to be there, while at the weekend I would have pages and pages of dialogue. There was a lot of pressure for that one day in the supermarket, the pressure was on everyone, crew and cast; we all worked extremely hard and every week, Sunday was a long and hard day. We'd start at seven and finish at seven. But I'd be up at half five learning lines, because while I might have only two or three lines in one scene, in others I could have reams of dialogue, a lot of which had to be spoken as we were on the move. Some scenes were difficult, some were easier. For instance, we couldn't show any of the items on the shelves in any detail, because of product placement rules; it was always irritating when we'd done a perfect take and then had to go again because the label on a tin of beans was showing. As this was a working supermarket there was a lot of work just to get that one shot right – and that was *every* background shot – which meant we had to run-through each scene before we filmed it, adding to our time on set.

Sometimes we had nearly a hundred pages of dialogue to cover in one day, and it went on week after week, as Granada really latched on to our double act. This was great, but it took its toll – the two of us felt a lot of responsibility to make sure the day went well. The crew and the director would change every week, so they got a week off; Ken and I didn't, we were there, constantly, for five years. Ken Morley has said, of that time: 'I turned mad and Kevin turned to drink.' Only I'd add: 'You mean madder than normal, Ken.'

I never expected to be at the centre of such a long-running storyline like that. After all, at the very beginning of my time on the Street, I'd only ever thought I'd be on it for just a few episodes. I had no career mapped out for me but I had expected to make my living working in the theatre, travelling all over the country to do so. To have the job on *Coronation Street* for so long was amazing in itself. I might be lucky enough to get a stretch of work blocked out for twenty weeks, and on a Friday night myself and Nigel Pivaro, who played Terry Duckworth, and one or two others would go out to a bar, have a few beers, and say job well done. To have such a long-running storyline, to have my diary blocked out for months ahead, was something I had never dreamed would happen. On the one hand it gave me amazing security and on the other, I found it quite frightening – I still had this fantasy that I was some kind of modern vagabond, moving from town to town. Having commitments for the months ahead, knowing exactly where I was going to be on every Sunday from now until Christmas, was unnerving.

I think I also carried on the drinking culture from the days when I'd first started. If I'd stood back I might have noticed that many of the crew were behaving differently from the 'old days', but I was set in my ways. When I started, we drank in the bar at Granada, at a local pub, and this went on at lunchtime and in the evenings. I was careful not to drink much at lunchtime but I made up for it in the evenings. As we entered the early 1990s, I found my drinking hardened me; I would keep it at a low level when I was working, but if I had a day or two off I would get completely trashed. Most people I know, grow out of the childhood drinking phase; I never did, I carried it on. During the summer some of the cast played cricket; husbands, boyfriends and partners would play too. One game finished with Tim Healy, Denise Welch's husband, as the man-of-the-match. His prize was a *large* Scotch in a glass, four fingers deep. 'Can I have a sip of that?' I said. He handed me the glass and I drank the lot, giving him back the empty glass. I thought it was hilarious. Tim looked at me: 'What did you do that for?'

To a certain extent on set, Ken and I had artistic freedom, we could make as much or as little of a scene as we chose. The reason it went on for five years was not just because it was fertile ground for the scriptwriters, bringing in love interests for both of us, or trouble between Curly and Vera Duckworth, but because we managed to make the on-screen partnership work. We both had tremendous fun and, while it's true I started my drinking phase around then, no-one but me is to blame for this.

The storyline had to end eventually, because it wasn't *Coronation Street* and it had become something else. Although it was a shame it came to an end, it was right that it did, because, as all the actors who appear on the show would say, there's nothing bigger on *Coronation Street* than the show itself. The two of us had had a lot of fun over the years. As we got on so well, some of the practical jokes we played on one another were pretty appalling; I tried setting fire to Ken's arse just before a live TV show in Dublin one time. Ken and I had been out sampling the excellent Guinness and while we were waiting to go on I took my lighter and flicked it on below Ken's rear. Ken was just starting to twitch when the interviewer started: 'Ladies and Gentlemen, would you please welcome on stage two of the funniest characters from *Coronation Street*, Mr Ken Morley and Mr Kevin Kennedy.' Ken ran on stage, hopping and jumping, closely followed by me, tears of laughter pouring down my face.

That closeness was an inevitable part of the way we filmed. The relentlessness of the shooting schedule meant that we had to help each other as much as we possibly could, no matter what our characters were saying or doing at the time. It was bloody hard work, but incredibly rewarding. Ken and I had a ball. A lot of the comedy was born out of our complete desperation – we might not be able to remember what was going to happen next so we'd look at each other, staring in horror. There was a production person standing by, ready to give us prompts, but we both prided ourselves on knowing the scene, so if we didn't know the line we'd both try to get an approximation of what was needed. If one of us ever had to take a prompt line there'd be ridicule for the rest of the day from the other. It was that closeness that made it work for us both through those long days; it was as if we were two of the Marx brothers, our performances were born of complete madness, of five years learning all those words, dancing the tango with lunacy.

One of the great pleasures of my life on the *Coronation Street* set then was the arrival of Raquel Wolstenhulme, played by Sarah Lancashire. Raquel was an inspired creation and Sarah was an inspired piece of casting. Norman fell for her charms, the only trouble was she didn't really fall for his; I think that was why the storyline was so popular with the viewers, they all knew it was doomed but they were as hopeful as Curly that he would win her heart.

Sarah was and is a talented actress and I greatly enjoyed working with her. That didn't stop me from playing pranks on her, of course. One time we were both in the Rovers; Curly had to open the scene, and then excuse himself to go to the loo, while Raquel had to go into a long and complicated speech. I left the set and heard Sarah start her piece, while I busied myself with the props I'd put in there earlier. I'd put aside a full watering can and a tin bucket. I lifted the can and started to pour, a loud clattering sound started and I could hear Sarah pause on set. I carried on pouring, raising the can up high as I did so and the noise of the water became a crescendo. I stopped the water – silence – then tilted the can forward and carried on pouring once more, back and forth from a trickle to a stream until the can was empty. At which point I walked back on set. Sarah, the consummate professional, was just finishing her speech, word-perfect as always, but having to avoid my eye as she knew she'd burst out laughing as soon as she did.

Later on she got her revenge. It involved a bedroom scene, some pillow talk between the two of us, and a pair of Marigold gloves. I deserved everything I got.

The storyline propelled Curly firmly into the limelight and I was on national television more times every week than ever; but being a recognisable figure had its disadvantages. Bill Tarmey, who played Jack Duckworth, and I were taking part in a golf tournament on the Isle of Man the same day we'd agreed to be at a 'Soap Aid' fundraiser in Liverpool. Bill arranged for a helicopter to pick us up from the golf course and fly us to the airport, where we could take a flight to Liverpool and a car would take us to the gig. Later that day this journey was to be repeated in reverse, so that we would be in time for the gala dinner on the Isle of Man.

Everything went very well until we flew back in to the Isle of Man's airport. When we boarded the helicopter, the weather deteriorated and the helicopter was buffeted violently in the high winds. The pilot informed us that the weather was too bad to drop us at the hotel, and that he would drop us on the cliffs about a mile away.

In high winds and pouring rain, Bill and I were left like drowned rats with the dinner due to commence in just twenty minutes. A little down the hill I noticed a small car parked, steamed up and moving violently. We ventured down and gently knocked on the window. It was wound down to reveal a bloke, semi undressed and sweating. A female voice from the back said, 'Who is it?' The bloke said, 'You won't believe this, but it's Curly Watts and Jack Duckworth!'

When Bill died in November 2012, I was one of many hundreds of people who went to his funeral. He was a joy to work with and I was proud to have known him and called him my friend. I treasure all my friends from those days; over my twenty odd years on the Street I never fell out with anyone on set. Some people I know find this odd, but there's an obvious reason for it. The set-up, the intense working conditions and the pressure that comes with being a *Coronation Street* actor doesn't really allow for feuds or prima donna behaviour, there simply wasn't enough time. I loved being on the show and I genuinely loved the people I worked with. Actors are very protective of each other, both on stage and on set. There's no doubt that people were aware of my drinking long before I was, and that I was looked after by the actors and crew. I'm grateful for that. Alcoholism, as I've always said, is the only disease that tells you you haven't got it when you have. As part of that denial, I hid my drinking on set. If I wasn't too shaky, I'd be fine, and I'd manage a few scenes before lunchtime. A pint or two at lunchtime was legitimate; at lunchtime I could go to the pub and then if I had a couple of Rovers scenes in the afternoon, maybe no more than three or four lines in each, I could get away with it. When I heard the word, 'Action!', certain things happened to me mentally and physically. Adrenaline took over. My professionalism took over. The skills I'd learned since college took over and got me through. I felt I was always on the ball. The only time I wasn't was when I hadn't had enough, and it was then that the nerves crept in.

I was drinking a lot once I'd finished work by now and some mornings I found it a bit much. I tried to curb my behaviour as much as I could but I would still end up feeling awful after a night out, and it wasn't until I discovered morning-after drinking that I found a solution.

One morning I was making myself a coffee when I caught sight of a doll of a Jamaican lady that one of our friends had brought back from holiday for us; you unscrewed her head and inside she was filled with rum. I'm pretty sure I made the obvious joke when someone gave it to me – that if you took off my head you'd find the same. Anyway that morning a little shot of rum perked me up no end and, as the 'bottle' wasn't see-through, nobody was any the wiser. My little secret.

At the time I thought this was the secret to life, or at least the secret to getting through the day alive. All I had to do was take a little sip of vodka and I never felt rough, I was back to life again. I thought it was the most amazing discovery in the world. I found out later I was what is known as a maintenance drinker; a maintenance drinker always keeps a steady level of booze in their system. Sink below that level and I would feel ropey, above that and I'd become visibly drunk. I could be fine, but I'd be drunk. My tolerance level became quite high so I had to keep topping it up. It wasn't a matter of binge drinking, I would steadily drink during an evening, I wouldn't even have to have enough to make me seem drunk, I just had to maintain a certain amount, which I would never need to go above, never try to go below.

To keep from being a noticed drunk – maybe even to pretend to myself that I wasn't really that much of a drinker – I would buy my booze in different shops, all over town. That way no-one would notice and at the same time I could pretend to myself that I was only doing what everyone else around me was up to. In reality I had no idea how much I was drinking – I really took no notice, as right then it wasn't doing me any harm. Or so I thought. I just had to keep track of my rota: where I'd been to recently to buy a drink, where I would be that day to go to next. When I bought booze in the morning from a shop, I had a stock of stories – it's my mate's birthday, I've forgotten to get him anything, I'll buy this birthday card, I know it's early but I've got my car outside on the way to work, can you just pop a half-bottle of vodka in for him? – As soon as I was outside, I'd bin the birthday card.

I don't know why the press never found me out. I must have led a gifted and lucky existence. I think it was probably because I very rarely did anything to draw attention to myself, anything to warrant that kind of coverage. I wasn't a nightclub person, I've always been a bit of a loner, the quiet guy in the corner with a story to tell, the bass player in the band that stands behind the front man and the lead guitarist. If I had an idol, it was the windswept and interesting type, a Gary Cooper type bloke.

The Bettabuys story carried on until Ken declared he had to stop or he would leave, saying that he was going mad. We finished with some wonderful scenes, like the time Reg was to marry Maureen and nobody but me turned up for Reg's stag night. It was beautiful, these two guys that were at the end of their tether.

As the drink took hold, I am ashamed to say that by then there were some days when all I wanted to do was say my lines in the right place with some sort of emotion behind it and go to the pub. I really didn't care enough by that point.

I wanted to put on a semblance of a performance but little more. More importantly, my drinking was now becoming an addiction, even though I wouldn't have known that myself then. The truth is, I thought more about drinking than I realised – how to get it, how to hide it. At the time I didn't notice and I had no idea I had a problem. Not yet, anyway.

I can't watch any of the episodes from that time. I have this image of myself I'd rather keep in my own head.

Chapter seven: cigarettes and alcohol

Romantically speaking, during the Bettabuys filming period, I was having a nice, quiet existence after the upheavals of my marriage. I went to Ireland quite often, sometimes with Ged, sometimes on my own. I might travel up to Drogheda and stay with my family, or I might stay in Dublin, hanging out in the pubs in Temple Bar. I'd become friendly with a few people from RTE, Ireland's national radio and TV broadcaster, and when I was in Dublin they would come and meet me at my hotel and take me out with them to pubs or to parties. They were nice people and I enjoyed spending time with them and their friends; I made sure I had almost no responsibilities other than getting up and going to work, and so I was never in danger of being too stressed about anything while I was there. I was enjoying my freedom. I knew inside me I carried a lot of guilt about what I'd left behind, but I pushed it away because I knew I couldn't afford to feel that emotion at that time. I was trucking along, waiting for something to happen.

April 1st, Bank holiday, Sunday night, 1991. I'd finished a long day's filming in the supermarket with Ken, and I was too wired to go straight home, so I thought I'd go for a pint, and maybe have a wander round town. It was a late finish as well, it was close to 8.30 when I finally left to go out. I went into one place, an Irish pub quite flash and piled high with leather sofas, but there was nothing on that night and the bar was already almost empty. There was another bar, Henry's, around the corner, a quieter, more relaxed place that I had been to once or twice so I thought I'd go in there and see if there was anyone I knew that I could chat to.

I walked in and there at the bar was the snooker player, Alex Higgins. I'd met him a number of times, he was a fixture on the Manchester scene and – surprisingly enough – a big friend of Stan's. I walked over, said hello and asked if he'd mind if I join him. I sat down to buy us both a pint. We started talking – although to be honest this was a fairly one-sided conversation as there were times (and this was one of them) when I couldn't understand a word Alex said, as he'd had more than a few by then – when two women came in to the pub.

I'm like most men, if I see a beautiful woman, I look at her, I don't know, maybe we men are conditioned that way, maybe it's biological. Anyway I couldn't help but look at this pair. One, an attractive redhead, the other, an even more attractive and younger version, but blonde.

I'd even gone so far as to say to Alex how beautiful she was when the redhead spotted him and wandered over to say hello. 'Hi, Alex, remember me?' He introduced us to each other and she reciprocated: 'This is Clare, my daughter.' Naturally I made all the right remarks about how she must have had her daughter when she was still in primary school or something, and Clare laughed. We started talking and all the while I had a running commentary going on inside me at the same time: she's beautiful, she's funny, I like her.

There was no pressure on our conversation, no expectation that it was about anything other than the moment, it was just spontaneous and lively. We spoke for a really long time, with me talking more bollocks than usual, just to make her laugh. I said to her, 'You've a delightful laugh, I like hearing it, I'm going to make you laugh so I can hear it more,' which worked a treat. Clare told me she and her mum had popped in for a drink before going dancing at a place called Royale's. Now, I don't dance – I do shake about a bit if I have a guitar strapped to me, but throwing myself all over the floor is not my cup of tea. However, she was too nice for me to say goodnight to and for that reason I asked if I could go with them. She looked a bit surprised but didn't hesitate in saying that I could. We went to Royale's and I bravely had a dance, I managed to not make a complete idiot of myself, and we ended the evening by swapping numbers. She told me that she was working in an exhibition at the convention centre, the G-MEX. I rang her a couple of days later, and invited myself to go in to meet her.

Clare was quite amused by the reaction of her colleagues, who were interested in seeing Curly Watts coming in to talk to her and I thought it would be a good idea to move on, so I said: 'I'm in the process of buying a flat in Didsbury, a new pad.' I wanted a flat to myself after spending all that time at Ged's. I wanted a place for a man, with a big telly, a fridge full of beer and some guitars. Oh and a bed in front of the TV so I can lie there, drink beer and play guitar at the same time. That was it, my man-cave. That was my aim in life right then, no more than that. 'D'you want to come and look at it?' I don't know why I thought she'd be tempted to see it, but luckily for me, she was.

We drove over to look at the flat, which didn't take very long. It was on the middle floor of a three-story building. It was a two-bedroomed flat, one of them huge, with a long corridor from the big front room past the kitchen and the spare room down to the main bedroom at the back. Out the window was a view of green trees, just beyond them was a house where Shaun Ryder lived, it was a very quiet area. I loved it because it was safe – a box among many other boxes. 'Oh, I can see real potential here,' she said. That was slightly alarming – I didn't want anyone having designs on my man-cave, so I thought I'd better steer her away from that quickly. We went for a Chinese meal in Didsbury Village, which I liked very much. I'd first explored the area when I started going there to hang out with Stan and his mates; it was far away from where I'd been living in Chorlton, and it was quite cosmopolitan. I found a local, the Barleycorn, which I immediately adopted and was in there almost every evening. No-one there treated me as him-off-the-telly, but as Kevin. I felt very safe there, very protected.

We started dating. I didn't yet own the flat and I couldn't take her back to Heartbreak Hotel, as it was a very cold winter and the place could be freezing. So if we were together we spent a lot of time in hotels all around Manchester.

We had a great time together, a lot of fun. We almost immediately started to do everything together. I became obsessed again, ringing her regularly during the day, I couldn't leave her alone. I introduced her to all my friends, starting with my mates in the pub. I didn't know until later that they were a bit careful at first, making sure that her affection for me was genuine. I used to carry a photo of her in my wallet, and show it proudly to people: 'That's my girlfriend.' I knew what they were thinking, they'd look at the picture, look at me, and think, 'How'd he do that?' I also met and really liked Clare's parents, Mo the lovely redhead, Harry, and her sister Rosalind. They'd all recently moved back from Saudi Arabia, where Harry had been working. Harry was very protective of his family but we hit it off right away and I found I could be myself with him. We could eff and jeff with each other and tell dodgy jokes. Her mum Mo was delightful, and I would sit and talk with her for hours. It was the opposite of what I'd had before; after being around constant conflict, this was a wonderful relationship. There was a lovely warmth about Clare, and her instinct to look after me. 'D'you want a cup of tea? Sit down. How's your day been?' I couldn't cope with it at first, I wasn't used to that level of affection – a little bit, perhaps, but not like that. I loved that I was getting looked after.

A few months later, we had become quite serious about each other and I was at work with a terrible toothache. The pain was so bad that I was taken off set and sent to a dentist, where I was told that my wisdom teeth were coming through at the back and the top. After some discussion, I agreed they all needed to be removed, that day. I was due to meet Clare that night. The dentist extracted all four of them, and gave me some great drugs to get me through the operation, so I was away with the fairies. When I came round he was chuckling away, and I hazily asked, 'What you laughing at?' He smiled and told me that there was one particular tooth he'd struggled to get out; he'd been pulling and pulling, and when he'd stopped tugging, for a rest, I'd said, 'Why don't you go through my arse and pull it out backwards?'

I was still off my trolley on the painkillers, and I was told to go straight home and not drink, but go and rest and try to sleep it off. 'Whatever you do, go home now, and don't go out.' I rang Clare, and explained what had happened. That evening we headed out to have a drink and, as usual, we ended up spending the night in a hotel.

In the morning, Clare left early to go to work. She had showered and set off before I'd woken up. When I eventually did surface, I realised I had bled during the night. The four holes in my mouth hadn't properly healed and there was blood all over me, all over the sheets, everywhere, it was horrible. I cleaned myself up and went downstairs to check out. I thought I'd better explain, in case someone thought something dodgy had gone on. 'I know you saw me check in with a girl, and there's blood everywhere, I haven't murdered her.' I pulled open my mouth for the poor girl on reception to look in, 'Can you see the gaps?' I was certain I had to explain I hadn't turned into a serial killer.

I introduced Clare gradually to my friends at work but then came an opportunity for us to travel on a works 'do' that Clare could join me for. Granada wanted a number of us to travel to Jersey for a PA, an appearance at a venue to promote *Coronation Street*. I tentatively asked Clare –

after all, this was a big step for her, going to a public event with me, so putting herself in view of the press – and she said yes.

I wasn't unduly worried about the press. Some things the press had printed about me in the past were way off the mark, but to my way of thinking – and I've always thought this – you've got to take the rough with the smooth. If you get into bed with these people, then sometimes it isn't going to go your way. I usually flew some way under the radar. I'd come in for a bit of flak when my marriage ended; Dawn and I had had to put out a joint statement which I'd read to some members of the press when I was stood on my own front door step. How idiotic is that, as if it's anyone's business what goes on in my marriage, I thought. But mostly I was able to keep out of the papers, other than the times Granada needed some PR done for the programme. For all the time I'd been seeing Clare, nothing had made it to the papers, which I was glad of for her sake.

We arrived at the hotel and settled in. The only commitment we had that day was to have tea in some old lady's house, which we duly did. The following morning the phone in our room rang. 'Kevin, Kevin, you don't know me, I'm a friend of your family's from Drogheda. I'm in Jersey right now, same as you.' I hadn't heard his name mentioned by my family before but I was happy to chat with him. 'Are you? Where are you staying?' He didn't answer my question, perhaps the alarm bells should have been ringing, but I didn't worry as he carried on: 'Yeah, so will you meet me?' I arranged to meet him and thought no more about it until I had to wander down to say hello to this stranger.

I arrived to find this man standing there, looking over my shoulder. 'Where's the, er, where's… ?' I thought, what's that got to do with you, and said so. A bit shamefacedly he said, 'Look, I'm sorry Kevin, I do know your family in Drogheda but that's not why I'm here.' It turned out he worked for a tabloid newspaper and he was here to cover what was to him a boring PR outing to Jersey, and had suddenly become more exciting when he'd seen me with a beautiful blonde woman who neither he – nor his news-desk people – knew anything about. I listened to him and thought of all the things I'd like to say, but I knew that would get me only vilification in the paper, so instead I said, 'Blonde woman? Who? Oh, you must mean my nurse.' He looked puzzled. 'A nurse? What for? What kind of nurse?' 'She's my Psychiatric nurse,' I told him. Clare did not look like a psychiatric nurse, whatever a psychiatric nurse looks like, and he knew something was up. 'Why d'you need a psychiatric nurse, Kevin?' I had my answer ready: 'Every good actor needs one.' I left it like that, which of course drove him crazy. The next morning he was waiting outside the hotel with his photographer, 'What's her name?' I told him. 'Kevin, what does she do?' 'You know what she does, she's my psychiatric nurse.' We went off to the function, and in the paper the next day there was my picture, with Clare standing next to me, and the caption, *Kevin and his psychiatric nurse* – I thought that was quite funny. Clare thought it was hilarious.

My Mum and Dad were very happy that I'd met Clare. Dad said, 'It's really good that you found someone else, someone to keep up with you.' I'd been taking him out with me whenever I needed company or to go on a trip and I think he'd found it tiring, particularly the drinking. At work, the storyline between Curly and Raquel rumbled on. It was funny that during the day I had to play a man pining for a beautiful woman, while in real life I was happily going out with one. Our relationship seemed so right, even from the early days, and we were never out of each other's pockets. I had bought my flat; I had my fridge full of beer and a big mattress in front of the telly. That's the way I wanted it. Gradually Clare moved in, spending less and less time at her parents' home, and more and more time with me. As women do, she surreptitiously started moving little bits and pieces about. Eventually I had to concede defeat and move the mattress into the bedroom, with a proper base and headboard. The fridge had food in – real food – and sometimes I had to move some of the beer out to make room. Both our parents came round to visit all the time, they got along fine and everything was rosy.

There were still times when I wanted to be away though, and St Patrick's Day in New York had become a bit of a tradition for me and Dad now. Before I went away, Clare said, 'The bedroom could do with a bit of decorating, you know,' and I looked about the room and said, 'Yes, you're right, it needs a woman's touch, doesn't it.' We agreed she'd do something to it while I was away, so off Dad and I went for another fabulous good old piss-up away.

When I returned home she told me to put my bags down at the door while she took me down to the bedroom to show me what she'd done. It was Barbie's bedroom; drapes, fabric swagged on walls and all over the place, hangings, you name it. I looked back over the front room and the fabrics were hanging there too. My man-cave had gone. 'Do you know what,' I said, as Clare looked intently at me, waiting for a reaction, 'I love it.' And I did – because it was now a home for the both of us.

Later that year I decided to go to America again, only this time for the World Cup. I was going to go with one of the other cast members, and with the landlord of a pub I used to drink in, the Ox Noble in Manchester. We were all big supporters of Ireland who, under Jack Charlton, had made it to the World Cup finals. I rang Clare at work and said, 'Listen, I've got something to ask you, it's very important.' She was very hesitant on the phone: 'Okay,' she said. 'We'll go out for dinner,' I told her, 'and I'll ask you then.'

When we reached the restaurant, Clare was impatient. 'Well, ask me, ask me then,' she demanded. I held her hand, looked into her eyes, and said, 'Do you mind if I go to America with my mates to watch the World Cup?'

I didn't think what I said was funny, but Clare laughed a lot. I thought it was nice of me to ask as we were never away from each other by then. I didn't twig at all. 'Of course you can go,' she said, and I loved her for that.

After we were married she told me she thought I was going to propose. I suppose it's quite funny if you think of it like that.

Ireland beat Italy, the eventual finalists, to come second in their group but lost against Holland when playing in Orlando. While in Florida I came across Disneyland, and I had to ring Clare to tell her about it: 'You've got to come and see Mickey Mouse.' Clare had never been to America. So later that year that's what we did, the two of us. We went for a week, and, as well as seeing Mickey Mouse, we also saw Kevin Keegan. It was while we were queuing to go on the Jaws ride, he was some way in front of us, and he'd just taken over as manager of Manchester City. So of course I had to have my photograph taken with him.

We had the greatest time in Florida, and we both really enjoyed Disneyland. I said to Clare, 'You know, if we have children, we should bring them here.' I didn't think about what I was saying, I was just being a normal bloke and saying what I thought – it just seemed like the right thing to say at the time. I guess by then I did know I was going to marry her.

She had decided to do some ironing one day, and came across my old Déjà Vu t-shirt, and wanted to throw it out. I explained that no matter how raggedy it got I wanted to keep it, and I realised I had to show her why. So I took Clare to Nashville. We went round all the sights. We went to Tootsie's – my card was still there behind the bar – and after I'd played a short set, this time on my own, I gave them a new one to put up. That night we hired a limousine, and went to Déjà Vu, to see the Fifty Beautiful Girls and Three Ugly Ones. We arrived to find it had all changed. The cowboys on the stools had gone, it had been spruced up to look like a bad 1970s discotheque, neon lights in tubes all over the place. It had lost all the charm. I was really fed up about it, and Clare went up to one of the bouncers to ask where the greasy pole had gone, and where the three ugly girls were. The guy simply replied, 'Ma'am, they're on tour.'

In Nashville, Clare and I met a couple of guys at a boozer called The Sherlock Holmes, where there was a picture of me on the wall. One of the guys was called Archie, and I pointed out my picture. 'You're joking,' he said, then had a proper look, and then asked us both back to his house the following day for something to eat. We went to Archie's house for a BBQ, only he'd forgotten to mention that he lived about four hours outside Nashville. He'd said the night before that it was right round the corner. Nevertheless we had a really nice time. We told them we were getting married the following year, and on our wedding day we heard from Archie and his wife – they'd bought us a brick. To refurbish a park in Nashville they were asking for people to sponsor the park by buying a brick that the city would use to pave the park.

Clare and I went back, years later, to see our brick. By then I was sober, and in Nashville I went to an AA meeting. I went back into Tootsie's, and my two cards were still there, but I didn't add a third. I don't know why. I don't think Tootsie's was the place for sobriety. I'll always love it, though…Work was hard going right then. I enjoyed it, but the pressure of the Bettabuys hadn't let up, and the storylines involving Curly, Raquel and Des Barnes meant I was having to learn a lot of lines, as well as be on set for long periods during the week. As Clare and I were enjoying our evenings out, I found I needed that early-morning nip a little more often. If I got up and felt really rough, a small shot of something on the way to work always helped. I rationalised what I was doing by saying to myself that I couldn't handle the pressure of not knowing all the words that I'd have to speak that day, and the drink took the edge off the panic. I got into the habit of learning the first half of the day absolutely bang on, and then, during scenes as the day wore on I'd learn the second half. At least that way I kept up with everything.

Discretely hanging on to a drink wasn't a problem, it was the size of the bottle that was important, always buying a half-bottle. Of course getting rid of empties is a perennial problem for an alcoholic. I hid my drinking by flinging bottles into bushes and things. Much to my horror, later on the council introduced the large bottle banks, where people could merrily go along and chuck wine bottle after wine bottle with no shame whatsoever, whereas I had gone through tremendous shenanigans just to get rid of the damn things.

No-one ever said no to me when I was buying booze, even though it was, strictly speaking, before they were supposed to sell them. Once, someone grassed me up to a paper, although curiously that wasn't aimed at tarring my reputation, it was aimed at the owner of the shop for selling booze out-of-hours. Obviously something had gone on between this guy and the owner, and to get back at him he rang the *Daily Mirror* – which in those days was edited by Piers Morgan, a friend ever since I was introduced to him by Shaun Ryder – and told Piers that I was buying vodka at half nine in the morning. Piers rang me and I told him that I'd been buying booze as a present for someone on the show, and the story never ran.

Piers knew all about my drinking. We had been to Dublin, and he swears – though I don't remember this – that when we were in Bad Bob's, I proved to him just how bad my drinking was. I went up onstage to play with the band – they were used to me joining in there – I grabbed a guitar and sang along. Piers tells me there was a break between the verse and the chorus, a guitar break, and as I finished a verse, I stepped nonchalantly to the side of the stage, threw up violently, then came back to the mic in time to sing the chorus. Piers swears this happened.

While Clare and I were very happy together, that didn't mean we didn't argue. Most of the time it was about my drinking, and most of the time she was absolutely right. We didn't regularly argue about it, but when we did I would say something inappropriate, which would cause friction and we'd get drawn into an argument. We were party people, and we used to influence each other – she was my drinking buddy, and in those early days of our life together that's what we were about.

One night the argument was particularly fierce, and it ended in those daft proclamations that never look good in the light of day. Unfortunately for me, this didn't happen – I mean, I saw the light of day, but by then it was too late. Clare and I had a massive row, and it finished when she said, 'Right, I'm going to go away with my mum on holiday without you. We're going to go to Egypt.' Why

Egypt? I never knew. At the time, I wasn't thinking straight. I was on one, I was furious. 'Are you? Right, I'm going to New York with your dad.' Poor Harry – now the argument had escalated to that stage, there was no turning back for me. I bullied him into it, telling him we were going to New York as if he had no choice in the matter. (I couldn't ask my dad as he was away somewhere.) I hadn't stopped drinking since the start of the evening and no argument was going to stop me. The last thing I could recall was being in my flat.

I woke up, and I could see from the décor that I was in a hotel room. This had happened before. Okay, that's alright. Maybe the argument with Clare had ended with me storming out and going to spend the night in a hotel. I staggered out of bed and headed for the window. I opened up the curtains and instead of the sight of the city centre, there was New York. On the street below were yellow cabs. How the… how did I get here? I knew I was thinking of going, but I don't remember booking the tickets, going to the airport, the flight, nothing. It was the first really huge blackout I'd ever had, it had to be twenty hours long. That was scary. I remember thinking, that was lucky, it could have gone the other way, I could have woken up in prison.

And then I heard snoring from behind me in the room.

I turned round and there was a huge lump in the other bed. Thank God, I breathed a sigh of relief, whoever it was, was in the *other* bed. A big hairy arm was hanging out. What is this? I carefully tiptoed round and peaked – it was Harry. What a relief!

When Harry woke up I pretended I knew exactly what was going on. I never mentioned anything about my blackout, I had another drink and pretended it had never happened. We just had a good time after that. We returned home after the holiday, and Clare and I made up. I didn't tell her about my blackout until I became sober many years later; I kept it to myself, it was pretty scary. I must have said to Harry that I would ring Aer Lingus, I had my route to New York through Shannon so that I didn't have to go through Customs – but I don't remember anything. It may well have been one of the very few times when I've played the fame card, although it was subconsciously. Certainly we were looked after at the hotel, the FitzPatrick, and I've made sure I stay there ever since when I'm in the city.

I didn't learn from the experience, why would I, I didn't want to stop drinking then, I loved it, it had been part of my life for so long and it was part of my life with Clare. A big part. I liked how I was when I was drinking, people thought I was up for a joke, a laugh, anything, and people liked me for that – and one thing I didn't want to be was disliked. I always had a good sense of humour and I used alcohol to spur me on.

On *Coronation Street,* I was as mystified as the viewers

as to where the Raquel storyline was going, I didn't know what was going to happen. Then the producers had us working in secret; we read the scripts and rehearsed away from the rest of the cast so as to keep this particular bit of the storyline a surprise. It was very secretive. Sarah and I were sworn to silence, and the two of us had to troop off to some dusty garage to rehearse. I was going to ask her to marry me, at least for the first time, and she was going to say no. She would then run off – that was the beginning of that part of the storyline. Following the recording of those episodes, I had a week off and Clare and I went to Dublin. That whole week I'd been going through the engagement stuff with Sarah, the proposal, engagement, ring, wedding and arrangements – by some form of osmosis all of that must have drifted into my thick head.

The two of us were in a pub, The International. I said, 'I'm sick of all this will-she-won't-she stuff, I wish it was for real.' Clare looked in surprise. 'What do you mean?' I repeated, 'I wish it was for real.' Clare coloured a little and said, 'D'you want to marry me?' And I did. So, in the middle of the pub, I got on my knee and I said, 'Yeah, I want to marry you.' To my eternal delight she said yes. Everyone in the pub had noticed and they all cheered. Someone rang the radio station and five minutes after proposing to Clare I found myself talking live on RTE.

People thought it was a masterful PR move. I got

engaged on the telly and I got engaged in real life. This created genuine public interest, and the TV wedding then being covered. I was hailed as a PR genius but the truth is it was all totally coincidental. It was just the right thing to do, there and then. The week in Dublin became crazy and I knew I had to do something properly this time. We were going over to Spain with our parents for Christmas and I wanted to make sure Mum and Dad were involved so they could be there when we became properly engaged. Clare and I drove down to Fuengirola, where I bought her a beautiful green emerald. It was perfect. We ended up buying a place down there later on, in Calahonda, a present to ourselves when I first got sober, a place to go and get away from everything.

The culmination of Curly and Raquel's storyline, and further evidence of *Coronation Street*'s ability to capture the nation, was when the two characters were finally married. The wedding had been shot months before and seeing as it was filmed in secret, the rest of the cast knew nothing about it. We even had another film crew, and after those rehearsals the two of us would have to come back and carry on with filming as if nothing was going on, where we'd do scenes where Sarah and I would be bickering at one another, although by then we were 'married'. The wedding episode was released on DVD the day after the programme, a one-hour special, and it sold one million copies, which is an amazing number for something you could watch for free on TV.

Raquel and Norman went on the QE2, it sounded like a dream gig on the phone – you're going on the QE2, you can take Clare, the story's about you and Sarah secretly getting married – but we never got to leave the boat, not even when we docked in Naples, because we were filming all the time.

Clare and I married at a resort on the Caribbean island of St Lucia; Mum and Dad had never been to the Caribbean, so for all of us it was another beautiful trip. We celebrated by going to New York for the autumn. Dad and I had a favourite bar there, and when we'd been in the previous March for St Patrick's Day we'd had a photo taken with the bar owner and two ladies from Norwich. When we turned up eight months later, Dad and I went down to see the owner, it was still early in the day and he was just opening his post, with his back to the door. Dad and I started giggling as we came up behind him – when out from one of the envelopes he pulled a copy of that very photograph. How he jumped when we tapped him on the shoulder.

Clare and I went abroad again the following year and I drank so much rum in Barbados I actually gave up drinking it made me so ill. I thought nothing of it until I came home and went to a bar, I had one coke and then fell over outside on the street. I was warned that I could have damaged myself by giving up the booze so abruptly, the body has to wean it out, I was told. 'You cannot just quit like that,' the doctor said. This was music to my ears – it was better for me to drink than not to drink, great. So my drinking got worse.

I had feared involuntary detox ever since I'd been on that boat on the Irish Sea and had run out of booze in the middle of a gale. My insides had gone into spasm, it felt like I was being pulled into my middle, from my throat to my arse, I was bent in two, I couldn't keep anything down. I was sweating and shaking, so hard it felt like I was vibrating. At least I got away with that because I could blame it on something else.

I would row with Clare and end up spending the night on the sofa. Sometimes I'd start the night off in bed and then we'd row. That happened more than it should have done, because like most drunks I wouldn't leave it alone. I'd pick an argument over something, and then I'd keep going back to it, until one of us exploded. I tried to get better. I even went into a clinic, but it wasn't any use to me; I had a few days off drinking but when I came out I went straight back on the piss again. Eventually, it would be Clare that finally gave up on me. Clare and I had been married for two years by the time she left me, and she was starting to get educated about my condition – she'd realised my drinking wasn't normal. Her leaving me had been coming and when it happened it was fuelled by the fact that she had given up drinking.

A lot of people in recovery, I would learn, talk about their final days of drinking as a time when the writing was on the wall, and that it was just a matter of time before they totally accepted the fact of who and what they were. That they needed help. I went to a clinic before I stopped drinking altogether; I still imagined that there was a way I could learn to control my drinking, and I still felt that drinking was a benefit to me, even though I'd learned by then it wasn't. I would say that rehab was for quitters, as ever making something into a joke because it was too unpleasant for me to acknowledge as truth.

The press showed a lot of interest in my first trip into a rehabilitation clinic, and we even held a press conference when I came out. As if I knew what I was talking about – which I certainly didn't.

My past is littered with my drinking stories. Some are funny. Some of them, I regret. I can't even remember if some of them are true any more. I never wanted the party to stop.

Chapter eight: August '98: walking tall

The car pulled up outside the Priory on Friday 14th August 1998. I had to be helped to the front door by Heather and Clare as I couldn't stand up. I was wailing and sobbing because I was beaten at this point, totally defeated. I have only vague memories of those moments, I was out of it because of the vodka I'd drunk very quickly, the booze had really hit me hard. I was wearing some combat trousers, a leather jacket I'd bought in Nashville, and a t-shirt. People dress the way they feel, and that morning I'd dressed for battle. I didn't take those clothes off for quite a while.

I was helped down the corridor to Room Four, right next to the nurse's station. It was like a hospital room with a little bathroom attached, and had no locks on any doors. The nurse helped me climb into bed, I needed her assistance as I was lost, I was in a dreadful state. I knew I'd reached the end, one way or another; I just didn't know what the end was, which was scary. I was in utter despair. I felt that despair more than anything, more than any physical pain, because now I'd been found out. The biggest and overriding emotion I felt right then was shame, massive horrible shame. The nurse gave me some sort of Valium to calm me down and hopefully help me to sleep. Everyone else, like Heather and Clare, had been ushered away, as no outside influences were meant to intrude while I rested. That suited me fine, I just wanted to be left alone. The nurse was going to stay. My old friend Kevin Lloyd of *The Bill*, had died three and a half months ago when he'd choked on his own vomit. Nobody wanted the same thing to happen to me.

I sank into oblivion. The next thing I knew I was awake and staring at the foot of the bed. Someone was down there and then I saw that the Devil's hands, elongated and twisted, were reaching up from below and trying to grab my feet. I screamed and started kicking out and then I woke up, sweating from every pore like I was in a Turkish bath. It was the first – and I'm glad to say the last – hallucination I ever had. The nurse calmed me down, I think she gave me some Lithium, and I was able to lie back again. That moment, that feeling of being hunted by the Devil himself, was the most terrifying I'd ever experienced, a visceral terror that shocked me more than I'd thought possible. Eventually I fell asleep, and when I woke up on Saturday morning, the nurse was still there.

I drifted off again. When I woke the next time, it must have been Saturday morning by then, there was someone else sitting by my bed. I recognised him. He used to run a pub, I even worked behind the bar for him a bit when I was at drama school, all those years ago. 'Hi, I'm Phil, remember me?' I must have nodded. 'I'm one of the counsellors here now. You're going to be okay, I'll see you on Monday.' Then he got up. 'Thank you,' I said, though I've no idea why. He left and the nurse came back in. She had a tray with her. 'I've bought you some food, Kevin,' she announced, but I couldn't eat. All that I could think of was my dreadful shame – now everybody knew I was an alcoholic. Not just my family and friends but everyone at work; and not just them but everyone who read about me in the papers. Everyone who watched *Coronation Street*. I didn't know then but all addicts feel this dreadful shame on being found out. Paranoia is common, too; less common was my egotistical view that 'everyone' was interested to learn about my addiction. To me, that was so important. I *knew* the press would be after me, now that my secret was out. After all, we'd not long ago had a press conference about my drinking – surely they'd be hovering outside my room now?

I found out later that both Clare and Brian Park had given statements to the papers about me going into the Priory. Clare had said, 'Kevin wants to get well and regain control of his life. He recognises at this stage that he cannot do it on his own and that he needs medical help.' Brian had added, 'We agree that, given the continuing difficulties, the only solution is an intensive period of treatment for his condition.' After that, the papers decided to leave me alone.

I didn't know that at the time though, and it just added to my total despair. How could I work again? Who would want me in their lives? Everything was gone. No feeling of hope whatsoever. Everything had collapsed – mentally, physically and spiritually. And my scalp itched. I lay there, until I couldn't lie still any more. Eventually, I got out of bed and put the same clothes on. They were the only ones I had.

I opened the door of my room and looked out, there was the nurse's station but they all seemed to be busy, no-one was staring at me so I ventured a little further, all the while keeping my eyes open for signs that someone was about to pick up a camera and photograph me. There was nothing like that happening so I shuffled down the corridor, following the noise and the smell until I came to a small cafeteria. It seemed very nice, the food looked good and the people I spoke to were very polite. No-one said anything about who I was; no-one treated me as Curly Watts. I hadn't expected that, but I was too lost to appreciate this properly. I tried to eat something, I knew I should try, but I couldn't even put it in my mouth. I didn't talk to anyone about anything, I just said 'yes' and 'no' and 'thank you', and then headed back to my room, and my bed. I felt marooned in my misery, a castaway on a lonely shore.

Somehow I got through the week, I suppose I was in a bit of a daze. I just sat about, watching the people around me. I made no contact with anyone, I just replied in the briefest possible way to their greetings or questions, I was polite because they were but I didn't want to engage with anyone at all. My fellow 'inmates', I thought I should call them, although we were all there of our own free will – were in various stages of recovery. Some had the same shameful look I wore and others were open and trying to be chatty, which I really didn't need at that time. I looked away, and avoided their eyes. Still, others just wanted to be kind, to see if I needed anything or wanted any help, or to offer encouragement. They said things like, 'You're in the right place mate,' or, 'Don't worry, this is the beginning not the end.' They were great, but I didn't appreciate it then, I still felt desperate. I made up my own mantra – *pick yourself up, dust yourself off, keep yourself going* – which I would repeat and repeat under my breath, as some sort of survival technique.

So far, each day the staff had been giving me injections because I was malnourished and severely dehydrated. I was on Librium, which spaced me out but stopped my body vibrating from involuntary withdrawal. Later on, when I became educated about the process of recovery, I learned what it was I was going through. This is what's known as the 'jumping-off point'. At this point I knew I couldn't live with alcohol, or without it. It's a very critical time in recovery, because this is the moment when you get a choice back, when you realise you've got to be able to say, No, I'm ok thank you. Some of the crisis I was going through stems from the speed with which the body recovers – it's amazing how quickly it recovers – while mentally you don't.

When I woke up at the start of a new week I was told I had to go to a meeting. Maybe because I was still a little spaced out from the Librium, or perhaps because I knew without understanding that this was part of the process to make me better, I meekly went along with what I was told to do. I'd surrendered to 'them', whoever 'they' were.

I went into this small room, with six other inmates, and was welcomed in by a woman who introduced herself as Win Parry. Win's opening gambit was: 'You're here because you are ill. You're not here because you're bad, wicked, or any of the above – you're here because you are ill.'

The heavy cloud hanging over me for the last couple of days shifted a bit.

'This is the beginning,' she continued, 'this is not the end. It is the end of a certain chapter of your life, but the beginning of another.'

I took in what she said, and thought, maybe I am ill. Maybe this is the answer. Maybe all the crazy stuff that's happened is because I'm ill. And if I'm ill then I'll get better, and then I'll be able to drink again. But this time, not madly. I'll be able to drink like a normal person. I've abused it and poisoned myself, what I need to do now is get better and go back to the way I used to drink, when I enjoyed it. Suddenly the world seemed a bit of a brighter place.

'Then,' she said, 'there are three things that are now your priority. Number one, sobriety. Number two, sobriety. Number three, sobriety. Nothing else matters. You're here for the next few weeks to complete the first stage in becoming well – in becoming sober.' She looked carefully round the room at each of us. 'Some of you may not make it.'

I took that to mean that some of us might not recover from alcoholism. But later on, I realised that Win meant exactly what she said – that some of us in that room might die because they couldn't stop drinking. And that's exactly what happened. Some of those in that room are now dead.

She went through what was going to happen in the days and the weeks ahead. What we were going to go through, how they were going to help rehabilitate us by changing our thinking. 'Honesty,' stressed Win, 'is the key. You've all got shameful stories to tell. You can't afford to go into denial any more, you're in it together. You're part of a group, and in that group there is strength.'

She explained that what we had to do first was to admit defeat in the fight to control our drinking. 'You cannot get in the ring with this again,' she said. I needed to be told I'd surrendered but I realised that was what had happened on Friday; I would have done anything just to feel better. And now I was here I wanted to show everyone that I was doing what I was told, because they said they could help me.

I'm ashamed to say that my ego was rampant at that time. I had very few things that I wanted, but among them was to try and save my career. I starting thinking that this meeting was something we could do in *Coronation Street*. This is how mad and deluded I was. I'll do this course, come back with my brilliant idea, the scriptwriters will love it – *Curly goes through rehab*. It'll be a great story, I can see awards, I can see everything. I can see it going my way.

Win carried on explaining what was going to happen. 'What we're doing today is talking about how you feel. British people don't talk about how they feel; you go up to someone in the street, ask how they are and they'll say they're fine but that's a lie. This whole experience, this recovery, is all about you expressing those feelings of honesty. It's about how *you* feel. To encourage this, you will keep a daily diary, a feelings diary. I woke up, I feel bad, I feel terrible, that sort of thing.'

I felt a bit rejuvenated by everything so far; the little pinprick of light that had shone on me when she'd explained

I was ill had expanded as she'd been talking. That meant a little of the old Kevin Kennedy started to emerge, and in any classroom situation I've ever been in, the joker in me started to come out.

Win said, 'You might do ninety meetings in ninety days. If you do that, and don't drink in between, you'll have a very good basis for recovery.'

I chipped in, 'I'd rather do ninety pubs in ninety days.' A couple of the others laughed a little but the laughter died in their throats as quickly as my smile evaporated when Win's icy glare was turned on me. She didn't respond but just stared. I swallowed, and looked away. I decided I didn't like her; she wouldn't play my game, she didn't find me funny at all, I couldn't manipulate her, so she wasn't for me.

She finished by reminding us all that the definition of insanity is doing the same thing, and thinking it'll be different. That this time it'll be okay. Alcoholism is the only disease that tells you that you haven't got it. This is why you've got to be honest about your feelings. As we were walking out I spoke to her. 'Can you tell Clare that I'm doing everything that you're telling me to do?' She replied instantly, 'I'm not telling Clare anything. Who do you think you are?' I was taken aback. 'What? Who do I think I am? Do you *know* who I am?' She didn't even reply to that but just looked dismissively at me, so I backed off from that argument very quickly, I could see I wasn't going to win. My dislike for her deepened. I decided to stay out of her way; we'd already been told that we had three different counsellors, so I figured that maybe the next one will be slightly more in tune with my sense of humour. Me, me, me.

I didn't know it at the time but Clare was going through her own recovery. When my dad had said to me that he was glad I'd found someone to keep up with me, I'd realised that he'd meant my lifestyle. My drinking was too much for him. It never occurred to me that it was too much for Clare as well, and it was only when I went into the Priory that Clare realised the extent of her drinking alongside me, which she later told me, was the only way he could cope with my drinking and decided to do something about it. 'In my mind,' she told me when we eventually talked about it, 'your drinking was destroying us, but mine was normal.' She admitted that she too had been to see Win Parry. Win had told her that when I had finished, Clare should come back for a full assessment on her own drinking habit. Clare said she was shocked at this, gobsmacked. She thought Win hadn't listened when she'd explained how she drank to cope, to stop being scared of me drinking myself to death. Win had said her response was not a normal response. Clare thought she was a different kind of drinker to me, but if she carried on, she was hurtling after me and if she didn't stop drinking, there was a strong possibility she could either kill someone or end up in a situation where her life would be in jeopardy. 'I challenge you to give up drinking too.' Win had said. 'Fine.' Clare had replied, 'I'd show her.'

We got ourselves a cup of coffee and then went straight into our next meeting, this time with Mike. He was older, very dapper-looking, possibly ex-RAF. He was lighter in his tone than Win, but there was steel in him as well. He told us his story. I listened but I didn't see that it had anything to do with me. Throughout the following week, other people's stories started to come out as my fellow inmates spoke out. I sat there and thought that these people had really been through it. I felt sorry for them. I didn't see that there was any connection with me at all. Even after a week I still didn't put myself in the same boat as them. I remember thinking, What a shame for these people, they look like nice people; what's surprising is they've all got good jobs, just like me, which they've thrown away. My three main counsellors were Win, Mike, and Phil. When Phil appeared, it was like a friendly face – I thought I'd be alright here, here's one on my side, I can crack my jokes again, have a laugh. But I was met with the same reaction, a coldness. It wasn't a put-down although it felt like a put-down. I started to get jealous because Phil was joking about with another guy, who was further along in his recovery than me. Phil doesn't even know him like he knows me, I thought, why is he treating me like this?

We had three sessions a day. The first session was from 9.00 - 11.00, then a coffee break; the second session from 11.30 - 1.00, after which it was lunch until 2.00, then our afternoon session, 2.00 - 4.00, before it was social time. After that we had to write our diaries. I'd not done so much writing since I was in drama school. It's all based on the Twelve Step programme, it was explained to us that we'd be taken through the first Four Steps in the Priory. As we were going through the First Step, I had to write quite extensively: how drink affected me and examples of how drink took over, and how I was helpless against it. And then we had to read out what we'd written the next day. I put a lot of effort and thought into what I was writing, although at first I found it hard. I couldn't remember when drink had overtaken everything in my life, it had crept up on me. I found this very tiring, it was almost like homework. I was being asked to constantly think about alcohol, about how it affected me, and the people around me.

When others read out from their diaries we were asked to comment on what we'd heard. I would make a stupid quip, or an irreverent remark. The rubbish I came out with was stamped on again so I stayed out of it, I didn't want to say anything if no-one was going to play the game with me. I realised very quickly that I could neither control nor manipulate what was going on around me, so I decided to shut up.

When I arrived at the Priory, they'd taken a sample of blood. I was taken aside and told that the sample showed I had cocaine in my blood. I'd forgotten all about the wrap I'd found in my flat, and I was adamant – absolutely adamant – that I hadn't taken coke. I insisted on taking a lie-detector test, but they said it didn't matter, that was probably during a blackout, that I wouldn't remember, but it was their duty to let me know it was in my blood. I knew that I had taken drugs in the past, although not much as alcohol was my drug of choice. On the rare occasions I had taken drugs, it was only to enable me to carry on drinking. That's why I made a fuss about them finding cocaine, as speed was the only thing that helped me drink more.

I still thought I was terribly important – if I didn't survive, if I didn't overcome my alcoholism, then the world would come to an end. I was certain I was being watched, all the time. I was convinced the press were in the bushes watching me, and I had to grasp the programme because I was the pioneer and if I didn't get this, then what hope did normal people, the man in the street, have? That's how arrogant I was. In reality the only pieces that appeared in the papers were those that covered my going into the Priory. After that, the press left me alone – it was my ego, and paranoia, that wouldn't let me think that though.

On the Wednesday night, we were all told we were going to an Alcoholics Anonymous meeting and then ushered into a minibus. This was the first time I'd been outside the front door and as the van drove out of the gates I nearly ducked to avoid photographers, but no-one was there. At first I didn't know whether to be relieved or a bit insulted. Deep down I realised I felt relief.

We drove to a church hall in Altrincham. When we arrived, the place was already nearly full so we all sat together at the back, united in our shame like a chain gang. Because I was still feeling paranoid – that people were watching *me* – I felt we were being stared at as we came in, the people from the fancy recovery place bussed in to sit with the regulars, like the posh kids coming into a rough school. I couldn't have been more wrong, of course, this was just my ego at work again.

The people already there started the meeting, which seemed to be about them talking and sharing their experiences. Win had told us all what to expect: 'You're going to your first AA meeting, you do not say anything, just sit and listen. Listen to people's stories, look out for the similarities in their life stories to your own, do not look for the differences.' She added, 'Do not think to yourself, for instance, if someone's story involved them going to prison, well that's not me is it, because I've not been to jail yet – because the key word there is *yet*.' She paused and looked round at us all. 'There are Yets that may come your way. I haven't lost my job, I haven't lost my driving licence. These are all Yets.'

I was scared of being in public so I was glad we were only there to listen and not speak. I tried to listen, but it went on for what felt like forever, an hour and a half at least. I wanted to go back, I was bored, I didn't feel safe outside. In the minibus on the way back to the Priory, I said, 'I didn't understand any of that. Not one word, they're all mad these people, very nice but all crazy. Not like us.' I thought the others would agree with me but they didn't. I think they'd started to twig what the process was all about far more quickly than I did.

When we arrived back, it felt like the evening had brought us all together a bit more. Instead of all heading back to our rooms to write in our diaries, we all went down to get a hot drink. I got chatting to a couple of people, and it was talking with them that made me realise I did have things in common with them after all. One of them said, 'Oh, my husband's coming and wants to see me, I don't think I can face that.' I said without thinking, 'Oh, I know how you feel.' That – I know HOW you feel – opened up the door a little. Of course I clowned about. 'Look at the state of us, the Loser's Club. We're a mess, but we're all together.' A lot of 'the work', as the counsellors referred to it, is done in the social areas rather than in the meetings or in the groups. We were all in the same boat – a metaphor we heard a lot more, because there is a lot said about the lifeboat in the meetings. Those sorts of sayings, the things that make more sense to alcoholics, like a day at a time and all that, were being drummed into us. They were printed on posters around the walls and we started to recognise them without realising it.

The next morning, when it came to the time for people to read out from their diaries, I found myself becoming very close to this group. I was still very general about my own feelings; I wouldn't let anyone get close to me, deflecting them with humour, as I still had a raging ego at this time. I was still full of shit, I had no humility and instead I had a very high opinion of myself. What I hadn't realised yet was that I was talking to people who knew every trick in the book because they were ex-addicts themselves, they knew it all.

We went to three evening AA meetings a week, all in different places, one of which – a place that became my favourite later on – was at a scout hut in Altrincham. Slowly, I started listening to what was going on. At first it was like being back at school when I would fidget and fiddle, look at my watch or the floor, work out how the floors were tiled, sideways blocks of wood. Eventually I started to listen to the stories, the human side; people who'd lost their jobs, wives, everything, yet these people looked happy. They were laughing, and I thought, this is quite attractive, I could live like this, these people are happy, not miserable. The process of AA is abstinence, and while I didn't like that, I was starting to think about it. One thing that had changed quickly though was that I had started eating regularly. Halfway through my first week I was ravenous, and looking forward to egg and bacon at breakfast, another new experience for me.

On Thursday morning there was a men's meeting, where I met Patrick. I asked him how long he'd been sober: 'Ten years,' he replied. I couldn't imagine what it would be like to be sober for ten years. Afterwards, we went and sat outside in the sunshine. I said, 'Tell you what, Patrick, you see that wall? I'm going over the wall tonight. I don't understand what's going on here.' He laughed, and every time I've seen him since then he's asked if I'm going over the wall tonight. I was in *The Great Escape,* I was in *One Flew Over the Cuckoo's Nest* – I was in a movie, and I was scheming. I quite liked the idea of being mad or insane because it was more bohemian than just being a drunk. The truth, though, was that I was going nowhere. The real world was out there and I couldn't face that. I'd phoned Clare, and her tone was not friendly. She was glad I was in there, and wanted me to complete the programme, she said I should stay in there. It was a great encouragement to me that the tone of her voice by the end of the call had softened a little bit but I still felt alone. I hated where I was and the reason I hated it was because it was starting to work, they were making me look at myself and I didn't like it.

I'd been told I'd been written out of *Coronation Street* for the moment, and not to worry about anything for now other than getting better. That was a relief. Some letters from fans arrived, mostly really positive or sending prayers – there were one or two nasty ones, which I just binned. Harry, Clare's dad, came to bring me some clothes, as I had none apart from those I was wearing, no toothbrush, nothing. I couldn't see him, I was too ashamed. I asked them to tell him to leave the bag. Harry was understandably a bit upset, but I later explained to him and he could see why I was behaving the way I did.

In the second week there was a bit of a breakthrough for me. We were in a meeting talking about the Twelve Steps, and Win asked me, 'Do you understand this?' I said I didn't and a huge smile came across her face. She said, 'That is the first honest thing you've said since you came in here.' Something clicked inside me. I'd heard them talk about being honest, but I didn't know what it meant. When she put it like that, and that I was supported for saying it, I understood. Up until then I'd understood it intellectually, just not emotionally. I knew that drink was horrible stuff that would lead to my death, I got that, but I'd just felt the rest of this, all they were talking about, was nothing to do with me. At that moment the penny had dropped, and this is quite common in recovery. So when she smiled at me for being honest, I found myself wanting more of that reaction. These people knew what they were talking about, they could help me. It was my ego at work, clinging on to this honesty stuff to get that reaction. Ego can help in recovery, it's a strong thing if used in the right way.

There's a moment in every alcoholic's life, the crisis point I suppose, where they are confronted with the reality of their lives and their futures. It certainly hit hard, when it was my turn. To stop drinking or die. Like many people before me, and no doubt many others after me, rather than sensibly stop drinking, I had to work my way round to that moment. I had to clear my mind of the nonsense that alcohol had filled it with, and that meant I had to deal with what's called the Viable proposition; faced with the choice, I nearly plumped for the 'Fuck everything and run' option. The addict in me thought, I could carry on, what did doctors know anyway. Even though I'd lose Clare, and the job and everything else, at least I'd still have my booze. I could sit on that bench there – the old bloke made it look quite comfortable, and maybe in the summer I could go on holiday, and sit on a bench in the sunshine. I could drink, and nothing would bother me any more. Life could be peaceful.

Your addicted brain will try anything to soften the blow but there's no other way round it. That's the worst of it, knowing that the choice to live will lead to recovery, and recovery will be hard. Eventually, I had to decide to just do it – to stop drinking, and live.

On Friday I told the meeting it was my birthday. This was not how I expected to be spending my birthday, usually I had a good day out and a lot of booze was involved. Win said, 'What a great birthday present to give yourself: sobriety.' I'm not sure what I expected her to say in return – ooh that's nice Kevin, when we're done here I'll open a bottle of champagne – but I sat there, grinding my teeth, seething. I didn't want sobriety, I wanted a drink. I should have been off my face by now.

Afterwards, the rest of the group wished me a happy birthday but it was low-key. Later I heard someone else say it was their birthday. They were asked, 'Is it your belly-button birthday today?' 'No,' they replied, 'I'm one.' And a great fuss was made. What were they talking about? Why didn't they make a fuss about me? Then I realised: your AA birthday is the day you got sober, and your belly-button birthday is the day you were born.

Clare came to see me the next day. She'd stopped drinking and was going to AA meetings. She was great; protective and lovely, and happy for me that I was in the right place. I explained to her what I thought the programme was all about. There was a light in her eyes that meant my marriage was okay – a great relief. If we're together in this, we can survive. She brought a cake, which I shared round with the others.

Towards the end of week two I had realised that the possibilities of Clare coming back to me, and of me getting my job back, weren't things I could control. I accepted this and with that came the acceptance that I was an 'alcoholic'. I'd gone through the 'you're going to die' bit, now I accepted I was an alcoholic bit, which meant I'd recognised that I could never have a drink again. I realised I'd been sick, not been myself, I'd come to the end of it and I saw a glimmer of hope. The hope I now felt for me wasn't to do with Granada, or with Clare, it was purely to do with me – that was a seismic change – that whatever will happen will happen, because I can't control that. It's down to me. It's handing over. I accepted that Clare still loved me, just as I accepted that I might not have a job or a career when I came out, and that that didn't matter. That's when everything calmed down and I started to think and work on myself. Once I'd surrendered, a sense of serenity came over me. I didn't have to lie and scheme any more, a great weight had lifted off my shoulders. I didn't have to plan the next drink, or worry about running out, or go into involuntary detox – I could start to work on myself.

I started to appreciate the feelings of togetherness I'd discovered in the group sessions. Now that I had realised there was a common denominator between all of us – that we all thought we were on our own, and that this was not true – I worked harder in the meetings. I suddenly realised that I wasn't on my own, and that the shame I thought was personal to me was shared with a lot of other people. This realisation in itself was the answer as to why talking about my alcohol problem was vital to my recovery. It was the same for all of us.

I said in one meeting, 'I'm learning so much, it's really good. The only thing that's missing is the bar at the end of the room.' Everyone laughed, including the counsellors, because it was honest, I wasn't using humour to hide behind, or to impress anyone. I'd not realised you could use humour in recovery and it was very important to me. I started spending more time with the group, doing things together. Some of us had a bit of a kickabout outside, and I said, 'I know, let's get a league going. We can play a team against the eating disorders. That'd be easy, we could just shout, Oy! Yer fat bastard – and they'd just fold.' Everyone rolled about laughing. We were so used to that sort of black humour as the stories we heard in group could be very funny. We'd laugh because otherwise what else could we do but cry. Without humour, there's no recovery.

By this time the craving had gone, I'd got the choice back. It had all started to make sense – that smile from Win Parry triggered something that made me want to please her. I was people-pleasing, so I started to listen and learn more, because I wanted to please someone else, not just me. I wanted to please the counsellors, to show them I was a nice guy who'd fallen on hard times. I started to try and be as honest as I possibly could. In the Twelve Steps, you have to be as honest as possible, provided it doesn't harm others. I gained strength from imagining myself as characters in movies, like Randle from *One Flew Over the Cuckoo's Nest*. I had to be someone very strong, and very alone – which goes against the whole point of the thing, but I liked the idea of being alone, getting on with it myself. I wanted to be anyone, apart from me. I started trying to be like the people treating me. Because I did it for a living, it helped – being someone else has always been my saviour, one way or another.

The following weekend I was allowed to go home, just for one day. The nurse said, 'Look, you're going out today, if ever you feel, at any point, you don't feel safe, you come straight back.' I found that thought a big comfort, I was in a routine and this was going to be the first time it was disrupted. Clare collected me, and I was fine until we got on the motorway. I didn't like it at all, I felt very unsafe, there was too much unpredictable movement around me. When we got back in the flat, I felt safer and I decided I didn't want to go out. All the booze had been cleared, everything, including the West Indian doll had gone. Clare persuaded me to go and see the new house, it was half-built. I said, 'That's just like me, with scaffolding to hold it up, but on the way to being completed.' We were both excited about moving to the new house. It would be brand new, and that's how we felt our lives were going to be. When you're in recovery you're told nothing big must change in your life, you can't move, change jobs, don't get into another relationship, but this was different, we'd started on the house before I'd gone into rehab. We had a nice romantic evening in together that day and then she drove me back to the Priory.

It felt good to be back in the Priory, I even sighed with relief when I walked in. The demon booze wasn't there, everyone around me knew who I was, what I was going through, the stage I was at – I was safe. The next day we had a piece of work to complete before our next meeting, and I didn't understand it. Normally, I wouldn't have bothered, I'd have just given up, but this time I asked another inmate how to do it. I'd never asked for help before, ever. She showed me, and I realised that it wasn't a shameful thing, to ask for help. She didn't say I was stupid or anything I had feared she would say, and I understood that no-one was going to think less of me for asking for help. That was another big turning point.

The others in the group had also gone home for the day. Something had happened though and we were all called into a meeting. One of the women was looking very sheepish – we'd not seen her since she got back. The counsellor told us she'd drank. There was a silence in the room. We all thought she'd let us down, as well as feeling relieved it wasn't us. The counsellor lectured her: 'What was wrong? You've not been honest, with yourself or the group. How long did you plan it for?' 'I didn't plan it,' she replied. 'It just...' But he interrupted. 'No, no, no. You must have planned it. Where did this thought start from?' This went on for about twenty minutes. He laid it on the line, not just for her but for all of us. 'You will die. If you're lucky, you'll die quick. If you're unlucky, it'll be misery, and then you'll die.' It was really heavy, and this woman was in bits. 'Okay,' he finally said, 'everyone stand up and give her a hug.' We rushed to her and gave her a big cuddle. Actually, I don't think we were cuddling, I think we were hanging on. That was a big moment for all of us, I remember thinking, how fragile life was. And so it proved; two weeks after she left the place, she fell down some stairs and died. No-one said she was drunk, but that was what we all understood. It's no good trying to help the addict if they don't want help.

Our group decided we wanted a night out, and we all went to the pictures to see *Saving Private Ryan* but when we got there it was full so we saw something else – but I couldn't tell you what because it was the first time I'd been out in public and I felt people looking at me, staring and pointing. I thought I could hear them say, 'Oh, he's a drunk in rehab,' but not everybody reads the papers, or cares, so they might just be saying, 'Look, there's Curly Watts.' I shrank inside and tried to pretend it wasn't happening, but the others from the group noticed and said, 'Is this normal for you?' When we went into group the next day, in their diaries a few of them wrote 'It was a bit strange going outside with Kevin because people kept pointing,' and it freaked them out, because of the sensitivity they now had. I'd heard the others reading out their thoughts and I realised it wasn't just me, other people had experienced this – and at the same stage of recovery, of sobriety. I felt a sense of comradeship. They experienced what I felt – and they felt the same. I wasn't being paranoid. Another cloud disappeared.

Mum and Dad came to see me. We had a meal in the cafeteria. Mum was really happy that I was in hospital, that I was getting the help I wanted and needed. Dad was supportive. All I wanted to do was to tell them how happy I was. Later on, I realised Mum had glamourised my drinking; when she read they'd opened a rehab centre in Ireland, she said proudly, 'There isn't a rehab that would hold our Kevin.' I wanted to tell them that I felt ashamed of how I'd behaved, but I couldn't explain my sense of shame, mostly because I didn't know how to start. The shame I feel will never go away for me. I have a big problem with it. This is just me, not all alcoholics. I'll forgive anyone anything, but I find it difficult to forgive myself. Even today a piece of music will come on the radio, something I listened to when I was drinking, and as soon as I hear it, I'm dragged back in time and I feel shameful. Sometimes I'll go to a meeting and talk about it and sometimes I'll battle with it, until I'm beaten again and then go to a meeting. The important thing is I am dealing with it, rather than pouring a drink on it.

Week four, my final week inside, was a big week. I knew I was getting out at the weekend, but there was a couple of obstacles I had to get through first. The main one was Step Four, where you have to write your life story down, and then read it out. I got the feeling that if I didn't get that right, I wouldn't be allowed to leave. I wrote, as honestly as I could, four, maybe five pages of A4. Some funny bits, some sad bits; it's not like a CV, but that's how it came out, with all the drinking and everything, but I couldn't help that. It's my story. It's the way it was. I've done Step Four again, since.

Once I'd written my life story, I had to then write my aims and expectations, as honestly as I could. I analysed *why* I had been drinking, and I came to the conclusion that drinking kept me safe from people. I'm quite shy, I was fine if I was performing, but I never wanted to blow my own trumpet. It's as if I was putting myself down all the time. I don't know where that came from. It was a defence. I realised that I was talented and had a future, but I was embarrassed by it. I liked the idea of being very good at what I did, but not bragging about it. I wrote it the only way I knew how, as a performance piece. It was honest. I only had one aim, which was to stay sober.

I also had a plan – we weren't allowed home until we'd worked out what we were going to do. Monday, meeting at the Priory. Wednesday, meeting at the scout hut in Altrincham, if City weren't playing at home. Friday, meeting in somewhere different every week. Saturday off, for the football. Sunday, meeting in Altrincham. I thought it was a great plan, it involved lots of meetings, and football. That's what I did when I left. I still drove past my old pub on the way to meetings. I wondered if they missed me, if they were talking about me. I never saw most of my pub friends ever again, unless I accidentally bumped into them in the street. We were told before we left the Priory, that we had to change our playgrounds. People like Stan I kept in touch with, I'd go round to his house and we'd play music together. He never said much about what had happened but simply, 'You're not on your own, mate.'

When I came out of the Priory, I had things in my mind from the life story I'd written down. I wanted to see something of my past, before I'd started drinking. It was a bit sentimental, I suppose, but I drove back to my old childhood stomping ground, the playing fields of Wembley, the battlegrounds of Thermopylae. I stood there and it was too much. I got back in the car and started driving off, when I heard someone calling me. In my rear-view mirror I saw someone running after me. I don't know if it was Michael or someone else from those childhood days. I couldn't cope with the thoughts crowding in and I carried on driving away. The memories of what that young person was, that young kid and what had happened to him, the conflict, at that moment it was all too much. I don't know why I didn't stop and say something. I wish I had.

The next few months were mostly a happy time. I'd go to the Priory for Monday night meetings which were mostly made up of the same group, but now I could see how other people were progressing, and feel how well I was doing. I got to listen to what other people's lives were like, and thanks to that I realised I wasn't out for myself, as I had been when I was drinking. I wanted to know what happened to that person, how his day had been. Mostly I stayed at home, and didn't venture out a lot. Not long after I'd left the Priory I had one bad night when I was at home on a Saturday night. The phone rang about 7.30pm, it was the press officer at Granada who was calling about a story. It was very unusual for them to ring on a Saturday, usually the story is in on a Friday and they call you then so you can get a rebuttal in. This time it seemed the paper didn't want to give me that chance. They were going to run a piece about me smoking cannabis in the rehab clinic I'd been to before the Priory. It freaked me out. What shall I do? I couldn't even remember if it was true, it was so long ago and I couldn't remember much of what I was doing in those days. I rushed out and found a meeting to go to, to help me calm down. 'This is terrible,' I told the room, 'not because of what they've said about me, but because they're giving money to an addict, to say something about me. Money to an addict – what's he going to do with it?' I needed to demonise someone, anyone, and conveniently it was the newspaper. When the piece appeared, it was rubbish, no facts at all, it was just an excuse for a big headline.

I learned a lot about addiction, from being in the Priory, and also in meetings. Clare did as well. We learned that, with addiction, choice is taken away from you. I've talked to alcoholics who are crying when they're drinking, not because they *want* to drink, but because they *have* to. I found it frustrating when I spoke to alcoholics who are still drinking, because if someone said to me you need never drink again, I'd have asked why. Before I became sober, my goal was to be able to drink like a normal person. I didn't want not to drink again. What about celebrations? Birthdays? What was I supposed to do then? Now I know the answer. Sometimes, it's to say, I could murder a pint – but when I say it out loud, I've not kept it to myself, there's no secrecy, and that breaks the spell.

In a meeting, there are no leaders. There is a structure, but nobody tells anyone what to do. That's the way it works. It doesn't happen in society now – people sitting round in a room, being totally honest with each other. This was my medicine. That was what filled up the hole where the paranoia and the booze used to live – this feeling that I'm not on my own, and that I can talk about anything and ask for help if I need it. It was like the camaraderie I'd felt when I was with the band, but on a deeper, more personal and more satisfying level.

I didn't even think about going back to *Coronation Street*. One of the producers had been to see me, and explained what they were doing with Curly. They didn't want me to return until I was fully recovered, so I didn't go back to work for six months. All I had to do was stay away from the first drink. I enjoyed going back to football matches regularly, but I couldn't handle the tension sometimes, and had to leave early because I couldn't hack it. At that time City's fortunes matched my own, they were at the lowest point of their history, and slowly but surely we both started to climb away from the bottom. I'd go straight to the ground, watch the game, go straight home again. If we were away, I'd go with Clare and we stayed in lovely places, enjoying the time away together. My world became smaller; the fewer people I met, the fewer problems I faced. An innocent remark by someone who barely knew me could grow in my head to the size of a house.

I was asked to go and tell my story on *This Morning*. I

was very nervous, and that started with travelling to London on the train. I talked it through with Win; she had become very important to me, her views were vital. She'd become friendly with me, and with Clare. I didn't do anything without asking her. I even rang her up to ask what colour we should paint our new living room. When I rang her about the ITV programme, her answer was simply: 'Don't talk about the awful stuff, keep it on recovery. You'll be fine.'

I was scared to death to say the words, 'I'm an alcoholic,' on live TV. I still had the guilt and the shame thing. I stuck by the phrases I'd got used to saying in AA, and when I said the phrase, 'I'm an alcoholic,' all that happened was that I made it unanimous. No governments were overthrown, no rioting took place on the streets. Another massive cloud lifted off me. I'd told everyone and the sky hadn't fallen in. I finished up by talking about recovery, and they were gentle with me, so it was just about okay, although I was relieved to get back into the Green Room. As I sat down, one of the guys on the crew came up to me, and said, 'Thank you, that was so brave of you. I'm in recovery, and I was just about to go out to score some heroin. But then I heard what you said and I'm not going to do it now.' I couldn't believe what he was saying. The very reason why I'd agreed to do the programme in the first place was the belief it might help someone, and here he was, in the flesh.

The following week I did it again, only this time in

Dublin. I actually stumbled on the word 'alcoholic'. Dublin had been my party city, what would the people I knew there think? Clare was with me, and after the show was taped for broadcast we went to see my old friend Brendon O'Carroll doing his 'Mrs Brown's Boys' show. Brendon came on at the end and did a little speech: 'Ladies and gentlemen, we've got a very special guest today, Mr Kevin Kennedy who you all know as Curly in *Coronation Street.*' People turned to look at me and applauded. The fear lifted. I could have kissed Brendon.

We left the Gaiety Theatre and went back to the hotel. As we settled into the back seat of the cab, the driver caught my eye in his mirror. 'Aright there, Kevin,' he said. 'I believe you're on the dry now.' I mumbled something and wondered what he was going to say about it. 'Well, you're not on your own there, now. Christy Moore, he doesn't drink anymore, y'know. And then there's another fella, what's his… ' and he went through this list of famous Dubliners who didn't drink. All the way back to the hotel he ran through name after name. 'Kev, you're fine there now, you're in good company.' It was brilliant.

Looking back, the most important moment of my whole time in the Priory came in my third week. A guy was brought in, looking a right mess. In fact, he looked like I had when I'd first arrived. Seeing someone in that state made me look at myself, and to measure how far I'd come in that short space of time. I found myself going over to him, and saying, 'Look, mate, you're going to be alright. If you feel you've got a problem with drink, no matter how big or small, then you're in the right place.'

Chapter nine: end of the road

One afternoon, I was painting my bathroom. Clare was at work. I was still in my long period of going to four to five meetings a week, and I was worrying about what was going to happen in the future for me. I knew that Granada had said I'd be coming back to *Coronation Street*, and that Curly had gone off to Southeast Asia to try and track Raquel down; but until I had a date in my diary for my return to the screen, I wasn't going to bank on it. It had happened in the past, when characters had been off-screen for a while. After the public had forgotten about them, or the storyline developed in a way that ruled them out, they were never called back. At least, this is what I thought at the time. I'd already been to see Brian Park when I first came out of the Priory, and thanked him for saving my life. I'd also taken on a sponsor as part of the recovery programme. We were all supposed to find someone who we could talk to regularly, get advice about our recovery

240

from, go to meetings with. I asked Tony Warren, who was of course the creator of *Coronation Street*; he agreed to be my temporary sponsor, which was the right way to go about things in case it didn't work out between the two of us. We met up regularly, I was supposed to keep him informed as to my progress, ask him anything I needed to, but when we did get together for a coffee we usually ended up just gossiping.

Once we'd sorted out the new house, Clare and I put my flat on the market; it was the bathroom there that I was painting when I got the call from my agent. Granada had been on the phone and I was booked to be back in on such-and-such a date. I was so happy I cried, I must have looked funny, standing there with paintbrush in hand and tears pouring down. It was the relief of knowing, I was more tense than I'd admitted to anyone about the decision and now it was made. I was in. 'There's just one thing,' my agent continued. 'For insurance purposes, they need you to go and meet with a doctor first. A psychiatrist.' I figured that made sense, and I didn't have any trouble with doing that. 'They'll call with the details and to set a time up.' I got back to painting my wall until the phone rang again, this time to sort out an appointment time to see the psychiatrist. We agreed a date – he was based in St John's Street in Manchester, the equivalent of London's Harley Street – and then she told me the doctor's name: Dr Dick.

This is a test, I thought. If I start laughing, they're going to think I'm still mad.

On the appointed day I arrived and told the receptionist I had an appointment with Dr Dick, all the while trying hard not to smirk. I thought to myself, keep it together; don't start laughing or misbehaving, no signs of lunacy. If anyone thinks I'm nuts, then Granada may not let me back.

The moment came and I was called in to my appointment. I'd already decided how I was going to project my well-being and confirm that I'd made a full recovery from my collapse earlier in the year: be positive, walk straight in, sit down, look him right in the eye. I strode manfully in to the doctor's room, walked to the nearest chair and sat down, looking him right in the eye. There was Dr Dick looking at me, a sort of disappointed, almost hurt look in his eye. He said, 'That's my chair.' I'd walked right past the chair he'd put out for me and sat in his. For a minute I thought I'd blown it, but luckily I hadn't. Whatever 'test' I was sitting, I passed.

It had been a hard few months. I was going to a lot of meetings and they were working for me but I had had to rethink my life as so many things had changed. I had been informed I would probably lose a lot of friends and so it proved. I didn't fall out with anybody, I just had nothing in common with them anymore when the only thing we'd had in common before had been the pub. In its way though this had helped me; I had decided there was no point in looking back, I must look forward. I was taught that my life now had to be a bridge to normal living – if I made my life all about AA, then it was not going to work. I had to be able to be normal. That was why it was so important for me to start on *Coronation Street* again. Of course, the night before I went back I worried how the cast and crew would feel about my return. My fear, though, was groundless. 'It's nice to have you back, Kevin,' several people said to me. A lot of my problem in the first place had been my wish to be liked, and one of the things I discovered through being sober was you could understand and appreciate other peoples' feelings more easily. That's one of the greatest rewards of sobriety, the realisation that it's not about how you feel, it's about how other people feel about you. People rarely said, 'You're much nicer, I like you now,' but it probably was true.

When I went back to work, another one of my biggest fears was that I didn't think I was going to be as good as I was, I thought that maybe by stopping drinking I'd lost some of my spontaneity; people sometimes get frightened of trying new things and I thought perhaps I'd lost that freedom. I found almost immediately that wasn't the case.

My first scene back – I couldn't believe it – was for me to return to my house, to find there are squatters who took exception to my return and immediately chucked a bucket of water over my head. I came on set, to be ready to rehearse, looked at the crew, and said, 'I don't believe this, I've been dry for six months, I come back here and I'm about to get piss-wet.' The crew burst out laughing, it relieved the tension, immediately everyone was at ease. It was important to me to show that I hadn't changed. I'd just been cleaned.

One evening I was at the scout hut in Altrincham, which doubled as a playschool for kids. I was in my seat while a chap I didn't know was sat next to me underneath the window. It was coming up to Christmas time, and the kids who used the hut in the daytime had covered the lower windows with black paint and then stuck cotton wool balls on it, with Christmas trees, Father Christmas in his sleigh, reindeer, fairies, all sorts of things like that. They'd made a lovely Christmas scene. Above that was the higher part of the windows and that was blank as it was high up. The guy sat next to me couldn't see the top half of the window, all he could see was what the kids had made. Outside, while we'd been in the meeting, it had started to snow, a proper blizzard. I happened to look up, and saw the snow coming down, thick and heavy. I nudged him. 'Huh, you seen the weather?' He looked up and all he saw was the scene made of fluffy white cotton wool balls. I added, 'D'you think the buses'll still run?' I saw a look flicker across his face, a look of pity: oh my word, the poor boy. I wanted him to understand what I was saying, so I said, 'That's really coming down now, eh, it's starting to swirl, look, amazing. D'you think that's sticking as well?' The guy reached out, held my hand, and earnestly said, 'Keep coming back. Keep coming back.'

At the end of the meeting, we both stood up, and then he saw what I had seen, and he looked at me and smiled and said, 'You daft bastard.'

My first sober Christmas approached, and I was nervous, but prepared. It was going to be our first Christmas in our new house. In the two weeks running up to the day I did more meetings than usual. They were great because everyone present was thinking the same thing: they either loved it or loathed it. Our families came round to the house, and we had a nice meal together and watched telly. No-one blinked an eye when I said I had to go to a meeting. It wasn't just the two of us, Harry too had stopped drinking, it was infectious. On New Year's Eve I'd been to a meeting early, and as the clock ticked down to midnight I started to become twitchy. Harry and Mo were with us, and Clare said, 'C'mon, we're all going to go down to Liz Dawn's pub.' This was the first time I'd been back in a pub at night (I'd been in during the day to eat), and we four sat on a corner table with Liz and her husband Don. We saw the New Year in there. We were only in for a couple of hours, but it was nice to be out for New Year's Eve, and I felt protected there. It was a milestone. I didn't make too much of it because I didn't want to think I could go back into a pub again. It was still very early days. The demon was still hovering over my shoulder.

My week now settled into a new routine. I still made it a priority to attend meetings, as that was the best way there was of me staying sober. I went to City matches, sometimes with Ryan, sometimes with Clare. The fans, if they noticed I was there, would sing songs about me, Curly is a pisshead and all that. I kept myself focussed on other things, too. While I had been in my room in the Priory there was a picture on the wall of a white boat in a sparkling blue sea, and I thought that when I got out of there I would go on that boat. At a holiday exhibition, I saw what I thought was the exact same boat, and the holiday advertised on board Star Clippers was a diving holiday off the coast of Thailand. I knew I had to do this, so I booked to go on a fortnight's holiday at Christmas, and at the same time I booked some scuba diving lessons so that I would be ready for the trip.

Hello! magazine contacted me as they wanted to do a piece about me 'getting well', which was not a phrase I liked to hear, it made it sound as if alcoholism was something you recovered from and never had again, like the measles. Still, it was nice that they wanted to do something so I asked what they had in mind. 'Oh, we thought you'd like to throw a party.' That was the last thing I wanted, a party meant lots of other people drinking and I wasn't ready for that yet. I talked to Win about it of course. 'Why would I want to go to a party? I don't like parties anyway, and the only reason I went before is so I could get pissed. No, I don't like parties.' Win told me that I had to say no to the idea. I did, but when I spoke to them they seemed quite hurt and I felt a bit bad. I explained that it wouldn't be the right thing for me at the moment, and asked if they had any other ideas. They suggested I renew my vows with Clare. I thought that was a lovely idea, I was very happy to do that, even more so when they suggested that they'd take us to Mexico to do so.

There was only one drawback. They booked us to fly the day after the play-off final at Wembley. Manchester City vs Gillingham. I'd always promised myself that if City ever got to Wembley, I was going to hire a limousine, fill it with my friends and a lot of beer, and drive there for the game.

In the end I did hire the limo, but there were only three of us in it: Clare, another friend also in recovery and me, and definitely no booze.

Lots of old friends were in London for the game, among them was Mark Aspinall from the Youth Theatre who'd come over from Spain, and Nick Conway, also from the Youth Theatre. It was great to see them and we all acted as normal; they of course had pints of beer in their hands, but everyone knew that I wasn't drinking, so if they didn't bring it up neither did I. I respected alcohol, but it didn't hold any fear over me. I still didn't go into pubs but I could wheel my trolley past the beer aisle in the supermarket, that never bothered me.

At the game, I find myself sitting next to Noel Gallagher. As anyone who watched that game knows, it was a nail-biter and it was only at the very last minute that City equalised when Paul Dickov scored, sending the game to extra time and penalties. It was about as tense a time as I can remember and while I wasn't going to go back to drinking, I was a broken man. When Dickov's shot went in, I think I kissed Noel I was so delirious with excitement. When we won, I kissed him all over again. It meant Manchester City were promoted. More importantly for me, was its significance – it was a good omen for my future.

Clare and I flew to Mexico the next day. We were staying in Puerto Vallarta, on the west coast. Before we left, Clare had done some research and we had the addresses of a couple of places to go for AA meetings when we were in town.

Alcoholics Anonymous has lists of meetings taking place all over the world and all we had to do was to ring up the London office and let them know which city we would be in, and when, and they would tell us if there were meetings there we could attend. When Clare called, though, she pressed the wrong button and rang my mobile.

So when she spoke, 'Hi, my name's Clare Kennedy, I'm going to Mexico and I'm looking for a meeting in Puerto Vallarta for next week,' I decided to string her along. I pretended to be someone from AA. 'Well, okay, okay. Can you tell me, Clare, what you're wearing at the moment?' She sounded surprised: 'What?' I carried on, 'Do you wear clothes?' She must have wondered what was going on but answered, 'Yes, of course.' Trying not to giggle, I said, 'Ah, well, the thing is, the meeting I'm talking about is a nude meeting, and I just wondered if you could send me a picture of yourself with no clothes on, obviously we've got to see if you're suitable.' Clare went ballistic. 'How dare you! I'm going to report you! I'm going to… ' I couldn't stop laughing, so she knew it was me and she roared with laughter herself.

We set off to our meeting once we were in Puerto Vallarta. We'd asked for an English-speaking meeting and we'd been given clear directions, but the place where the meeting was held was in a grim part of town. Part of the speech we'd heard at AA was that eventually drinking would take us to sordid places. I said to Clare 'Well, drinking might have taken me to some sordid places, but recovery's not doing a bad job itself.' The meeting – the first we'd done outside the UK – was amazing, especially when we realised that everyone shared the same experiences, the same despair, and now had the same hope.

When we returned home I was called in to a meeting at Granada. The producers wanted to do something amazing for *Coronation Street* for the Millennium, but before they would tell me what it was I was issued with the instruction to keep this one to myself. The producers said, 'We've got something for you, you know we're coming to the Millennium, New Year's Eve broadcast will have to be a bit special.' I agreed. 'Well, this is a massive secret, we're planning a two-hander – Raquel will be coming back for a special, just you and Sarah – no-one else knows. So you'll be back to filming in secret all over again.' They had decided to bring Raquel back, to break the news to Curly that they have a child together. I rang Sarah: 'I don't believe this, what is it about you and me and dusty garages?' The two of us were called to the producer's house to do the first read-throughs. The producer's dog took a bit of an interest in sniffing us and then settled down to watch as we plonked ourselves on his sofa to read the scripts. We were halfway through the read-through, approaching the really crucial point – I'm meeting my three-year old daughter, it was all getting very emotional and we were both quite wound up – when suddenly, like a heavy chainsaw, the dog snored as loudly as I've ever heard anyone snore. The scene was a very tough one to get through, it was strong emotionally, and when we'd finished, I said that I thought I'd need a meeting after this. Sarah splurted her tea out her nose. I'd never seen anyone actually do that before.

I really enjoyed working with Sarah again. She was very supportive and happy for me. I'd learned humility, and I was humbled that she wanted to do this with me, and finish our story. Gratifyingly, the TV audience felt likewise.

There was another distraction. The success in the charts a couple of years before of the two actors-turned-singers, Robson Green and Jerome Flynn, had started the idea that there was musical talent lurking in the cast lists of British TV soaps. I suppose they thought the actors would have a ready-made audience, and it was likely many of them would have had some musical training as well. Daran Little, who'd worked on *Coronation Street* for years, first as an archivist and then as a writer (winner of a BAFTA for his drama *The Road to Coronation Street,* based on Tony Warren's revolutionary efforts to get a kitchen-sink drama series on screen), was asked to see if any of the actors on the programme could come up with a song. I had a chat with Stan and he found me someone to work with. Together we recorded a rough demo of a song called 'Bulldog Nation', in a small studio in Hale. Darren thought it was great and sent it down to London to the person who'd asked for it – Simon Cowell.

There was a lot of umming and ahhing about it. Stan and I said that when you went to a record company it was usually to A&R men, but we should call them Umm and

Ahh men. I felt we needed to push the idea along a little so Darren and I had lunch with Simon and Denise Bateson, who worked for the record label. Simon depended on her musically – he's probably the best there is at marketing and selling, but he depends on other people to pick the right song for the right artist, and Denise was that person. We met in the Landmark Hotel. Simon wasn't yet God so we met in the coffee bar and discussed whether or not they should sign me. Simon was charming but all business; you could see the underlying steel there. What experience did I have of the music industry, they wondered. Had I ever been in a band before? Well, I said that when I was young I was in an early incarnation of The Smiths. It's not often when you see people lost for words. After a brief discussion, he said those magic words: 'Right, let's do it.' I signed with BMG, and so became another in the line of rock stars in recovery.

I trusted Simon immediately. He was very convincing and authoritative. He knew what he was talking about, and delivered that with such conviction that you thought he was right. With him, there was no grey area. Normally if I spoke to a director about a piece of dialogue, I could argue my point, but with Simon there was no artistic leeway. 'We're going to do it this way,' he would say.

When I see Simon now, criticising or helping acts, he hasn't changed one bit, he's exactly the same as he was with me. That's a credit to him. He would say the same things to me about 'Bulldog Nation', and what he didn't like about it, which for him was really about the way he was going to market it. We recorded a video of one of the songs, I wore mostly denim – jeans, shirt, jacket – with a black t-shirt and black sneakers. Simon took one look and said, 'No, no, no, no, that doesn't look right – we'll have to get a stylist in.' The stylist draped us all in beige, which *really* didn't suit me, but I trusted Simon so much that if he thought it was right, then fine. Once the record was underway, we never saw him again.

The whole thing about record marketing is timing and no-one seemed prepared to see Simon's vision. Unfortunately this dragged along while I was in Mexico; meanwhile I started working on the *Coronation Street* story with Raquel's return. No-one else knew about that storyline, including Darren, but I knew that once that became public knowledge then the record company would want to go ahead with the song.

I was also doing my diving training. Our trip to the warm waters of the South China Seas was looming and I wanted to be ready for it. So what with filming the regular parts of the show – then secretly rehearsing and filming with Sarah – and diving, I was keeping myself very busy. Wherever I was, I went to a meeting as everything had to fit around meetings. I embraced it, I felt I was getting the rewards. When I went through the programme with

AA I was told I wasn't going to get a bigger car, a bigger house, a better job, I was going to get serenity. I got that in spades. But I was also getting all these other things coming my way. On the spiritual side, I was happy as can be and on the working side I was equally fulfilled, especially as the emphasis seemed to be on the output of my artistic side. While I was in the studio I'd decided to record some songs for Clare as a surprise gift to her, the only person who knew what I was up to was Win and she had to deflect a few worried remarks from other people, as I couldn't tell anyone where I was disappearing off to when I was making the record for Clare. For her Christmas present, I recorded the Everly Bros tunes, 'Let It Be Me', while on the B-side I recorded 'Ride On' by Christy Moore.

I qualified as a scuba diver with a great sense of achievement, on 10th Dec 1999, in a freezing quarry in Lancaster. The next dive I did was in tropical waters. We went about six hundred yards offshore and I was only underwater for about half an hour but the experience was amazing. Clare said to me later that I didn't speak for about an hour after I came back on board. The two of us saw in the new millennium on the beach in Phuket, watching the incredible fireworks displays with happy, celebrating Thais, and an elephant in full Thai ceremonial gear.

The experience was all about new beginnings for me. I'd just done something new that I'd never done before which was diving. I'd recorded a song that might make it out into the stores and I'd just recorded the two-hander with Sarah, which had gone out over the New Year, to bring *Coronation Street* into the new millennium. They'd never done a two-hander before, ever. City were doing well, they'd gone up a league. Everything was rosy.

'Bulldog Nation' was eventually released – I think I mean smuggled out – in June 2000, and did well, but not as well as the Robson and Jerome records; and the idea of manufacturing pop stars from soap stars stopped. Later on, people would take me aside, make sure no-one was listening, and tell me they liked the guitar-led song but wouldn't admit to it. I'd become a secret pleasure at last.

On the strength of the record going gold in New Zealand, which meant it took on a cult reputation, I was asked to do a small tour of the South, playing with a US-based band. We started at the Riverfest at Little Rock in Arkansas – a place mainly famous for being Bill Clinton's birthplace and the site of the first racially-integrated school. The day before, I'd been filming a scene for *Coronation Street* in a park in Wythenshawe, dressed as a roundhead. What a contrast. I was now playing on the same bill as Trick Pony, and the great Steve Earle. The second gig was in Clarksdale at Morgan Freeman's blues club, Ground Zero. A huge hall with the best sound system money could buy, two huge bars, wooden seats, and – as is common in honky-tonks –

more graffiti than you can shake a stick at. Oddly enough, the stage is no bigger there than in Tootsie's or, indeed, any of the Irish pubs in Manchester. The third and final gig was in Memphis. The venue was a classier honky-tonk on Beal Street called Elvis Presley's Memphis, which has now sadly gone, like most of my venues. This evening was special, after I'd played and the band had packed up and left, I managed to find a midnight showing of the first Spiderman film that day it opened. I was walking home when it finished, glad I'd seen it before anyone else at home, when I passed an Irish bar and discovered that Ireland was about to kick off in their first game in the World Cup in Japan. All in all a wonderful evening.

Everything was great, but I knew there was something else we both wanted. Clare and I realised that we wanted children.

It wasn't as simple as all that, of course. All the years of drinking had caused havoc and so after a visit to the specialist where I was told I had been diagnosed with 'lazy sperm', we decided to give IVF a go. I couldn't shake off the image of my sperm lying about on deckchairs, not bothered and waving 'whatever' rather than getting on with their job. We didn't hesitate when the doctor asked if we wanted to have IVF, we both said yes simultaneously. The IVF process was difficult for Clare, it's quite invasive, and my mum helped us. As part of the procedure, Clare had to have injections at certain times, and as my mum's a trained nurse she came round to administer those to Clare. That was lovely because it meant we were all part of it.

No-one else was included in my little contribution. I was given a cup and shown into a room with what looked like the world's first-ever porn mag. It was that old. It didn't help matters when I dropped the cup I was supposed to be handing over – I had visions of my child being born with a bristly chin made up of nylon from the carpet sweepings.

I had learned in recovery that I had to accept certain situations. That I could not spend my time regretting what I had done when I was drinking. IVF was the next step down the road, and there was no point in feeling guilt; no panic, no finger-pointing. Clare too was going through recovery, and she understood this. The beautiful thing about recovery was that we were going through it together. We were both newly sober, and we'd been given another chance in our marriage. I should have been dead, or insane. I was given another chance. That overrode everything.

At that time, I was working with the lovely Angie Lonsdale, who played policewoman Emma Taylor on *Coronation Street*. We were filming one day when the two of us were asked to go up and see one of the producers, Kieran Roberts, in his office. We speculated as we went upstairs to see him as to what it might be – a new storyline perhaps?

Neither of us was prepared for the bombshell that followed.

'Look, I need to tell you that we may be... phasing your two characters out. We've not made a final decision yet, but I want you to know now that in a couple of months' time we might not be renewing your contracts.'

We were both absolutely stunned and left his office in silence. Of course we were expected downstairs, we had to go back to work. I took the director to one side and explained the situation to him, and how we were not quite sure where we were. We had a difficult afternoon. Angie and I clung together, literally, wondering what we were going to do. My biggest fear of all time had been that my drinking might cost me my job and now here I was, losing it and sober.

It was a difficult evening and night. I told Clare what had happened as soon as I got home, of course, but I couldn't sleep – I had no-one to talk about my situation with as I no longer had an agent. The following day I went up to some of the other cast members and told them the news. They were as shocked as we were. 'No, they'll never get rid of you, Kevin, don't be silly. Angie, yes, we can see how that might happen, unfortunate as it is, we don't want to lose a good cast member – but you? Never.'

I rang Win and went to see her. I'd learned by now to ask for help, which I'd never have done in the past. I asked her what I should do. She explained it would be like a bereavement – that I would have to grieve for the loss, but I had to accept that part of my life was over.

For the next few weeks I had the sword of Damocles hanging over my head. It wasn't made any easier by the fact that the first go at IVF had failed, which was devastating for both of us, Clare especially. We waited for the next cycle and tried again.

To cope with all this stress I went to a lot of meetings, but I didn't talk openly about either the job or the IVF because both things were in their own way hush-hush. Instead I talked with the people I trusted most. They all said the same thing, that it was a brilliant opportunity for me to spread my wings. I hadn't seen it that way.

I went to Liverpool one day to see Brendan O'Carroll in his show. Afterwards I went backstage to see Brendan and was chatting with him when my mobile rang. It was Clare: 'Are you sitting down? I've just done the test... I'm pregnant.' I was so stunned I said, 'Congratulations.' I think if she'd told me face to face I'd have shaken her hand, I was so surprised. I blathered something to her and then told the boys in the dressing room, who wondered what was going on. 'We're having a baby!' A bottle was produced and they all had a drink to celebrate the news – I had water – and then I went home to see the mum-to-be.

The next day I went into work still walking on air. The whole thing about recovery is about feelings, having them, expressing them. I was euphoric, the fear I'd felt had been overtaken by this feeling. Even today the memory of how I felt then still brings a smile to my face. I was summoned to Kieran's office again. I can't remember what he told me because it was all a bit of a blur – I wanted to tell him my news, how happy I was, but of course it was too early to tell everyone, especially as we'd not yet told anyone in the family, so I just sat there with this stupid grin on my face and listened to these phrases crashing over me. *The decision has been made... the press office has been told...* To be fair to Kieran, he was upset and didn't want the character to leave the show, 'But I have to do what the writers want to do. We're not going to renew your contract.'

I was fine about it, I didn't argue with him at all; it didn't dawn on me that twenty years was coming to an end. Although I was scared, everything was new and I was sober enough to realise that the glass was half-full. I was just so excited, so happy about this new life.

When I left Kieran's office, Alison Sinclair and the press office team were waiting out there, and were very businesslike. 'We've got to release a statement, Kevin,' they told me. They were just doing their job and they wanted to make sure it was right, that it was managed properly, and that I was happy. The agreed statement was all about the decision being mutual, about new opportunities for me.

I then had to go downstairs and have my photograph

taken in a large shot of the whole cast, which I thought was a mistake as it would be out of date immediately, but I went through with it. The rumour went round that I was leaving and all the cast were marvellous and supportive with me. Outside the gates there were loads of photographers waiting and I said a few words before heading home.

And that was it.

I still had a few weeks to go before the end of my contract, I had to have an exit storyline and so I was still around the place. Thinking about that time now, I realise the management wanted to let me down lightly. I think the whole two-month period while they were waiting to tell me the character's future was designed to give me time to adjust to the possibility, maybe even to make some plans of my own. I was a bit stunned, and went into a period of mourning, but it wasn't all over, forever. I was told I wasn't going to be killed, there was an option there for me to return to the *Street* if the writers found a suitable storyline. They had to do what they did, in the end, and I'm friends with Kieran to this day.

I finished filming four weeks before my last episode was to be screened. As soon as my last scene was finished the crew broke out into applause, and several presents appeared. It was touching, and not at all sad. I hate goodbyes at the best of times, so as soon as we could, Clare and I went to Spain. I had the same sense of freedom as when I became sober; I am very grateful for that part of my life and what it gave me. I was sad that it was over, but I was also looking forward to chilling out over the summer months in Spain, and watching Clare's tummy grow. I had some time. That's that. What's next?

My last episode was broadcast on 1st September 2003. After I'd driven off-screen, the moon and stars were shown high above the Rovers – a reference to Curly's love of astronomy. A really lovely touch, I thought.

Chapter ten: never fear tomorrow

The moment I knew my contract was not going to be renewed, I had gone straight down to the Casting Offices for Granada, and said to the woman in charge, 'Look, I'm getting the push from Coronation Street... ' She had interrupted, thinking I wanted to stay on, 'I can't help you on that.' So I explained: 'No, no, I don't want that, I want to know what's coming up, what's in production.' I was already in that frame of mind, I wanted to know what was next. 'I need to go forward.' She replied that there was nothing at the moment, but there might be something. 'Now, what should I do?' I said to Clare once I'd left the set forever. 'First thing I've got to do is get an agent. Oh no, the first thing I've got to do is get a pantomime.' A pantomime would give me something to look forward to. I had little time to get ready as the panto season was only a couple of months away and my first job was very important – I wanted to say, 'It's alright, I've got a panto,' as everyone knew that pantos were very lucrative. I got a part in *Aladdin* in Brighton.

That was a good start but I needed to get long-term work. I thought it would be a good idea for me to get back on stage. I spoke to Denise Welch, who I was very good friends with even though we had only shared a small amount of screen time together. Clare and I spent a lot of time with Denise and Tim, and she recommended her agent, Barry Burnett. He persuaded me to think about musical theatre and already had something in mind. 'Would you fancy doing *The Rocky Horror Show*?' I've always liked that show so I immediately said yes. He explained that the show was on tour so I would join the tour almost immediately and share the role of Narrator with Lionel Blair.

This would be my first musical and although I still had a strong sense of theatre etiquette, I hadn't ever been in rehearsal for a musical. When I arrived for the first day of rehearsal, everyone started warming up and the room resounded to several voices chanting out, 'Ma-ma-ma, me-me-me, mo-mo-mo...' I started laughing, I had to put my hand over my mouth, what are they doing? It took me a moment to realise they were warming their voices up, to try and sing without doing any damage to their voice so this was very serious, but I still found it funny.

My first moment on stage came when the Narrator walks out carrying a large book, from which he would read: 'I would like, if I may, to take you on a strange journey… ' Johnny Wilkes played Frank N. Furter. It was like a new world. I watched and learned how the show was put on, how they handled the phrasing, the swing from one section to another. It was like starting theatre all over again, only this time a part of theatre I'd never come across before. Even so, all my old training started to come back and being amongst a company was great fun after being on a television set for so long. I had lost a lot of the sorts of social skills you need in a company; mixing with the same people all the time, day after day, week after week, this new experience was very stimulating. Perhaps because I didn't have to be drunk to enjoy it, but maybe also because after so many years on set I could tell you where I was going to be on any given Monday, Tuesday, Friday at 3pm. I knew exactly which chair I'd be sitting in. The night my last episode on *Coronation Street* was screened, I was eating a meal in a pub with the director of Rocky Horror, going over my part. I could see the TV was on although the sound was off. I watched my last scene but it was like it was happening to someone else. The perspective I'd gained when I got sober allowed me to see outside the bubble I'd been in for so long – and I thought, I'm so glad I'm here, now. I can prove to everyone, myself included, that I won't go under, now that I've left it behind me. The director looked round to see what I was staring at, and said, 'Is that your last one? Oh, ok. Anyway... ' and we went back to talking about the show.

Only a couple of days later, I walked out on stage for the first time in years. September 4th also happened to be my birthday, and I prayed that the audience at the Bristol Hippodrome would be forgiving. When I was younger I had had a bit of stage fright, nothing serious but certainly nothing I expected to recur. Even though I was what would be called 'a seasoned actor' I had a full-blown attack of stage fright. My knees shook, but as I walked on clasping my book, I felt that fear disappear as the audience generously cheered and clapped my every line.

While I'd been rehearsing for the show they'd put me up in a flat on London's South Bank. Clare had come to visit; she was getting bigger by the day, and more and more boxes of small outfits were starting to arrive. She planned to return home to Manchester when I went on tour. While she was with me I had a call from my agent Barry asking if I wanted to audition for *Chicago*. Clare and I really started to think about the future here; there was great potential here for me in musical theatre. I felt a mixture of excitement and positivity – the positivity in particular came from my sobriety and I knew I could do this. I was starting to understand how musical theatre worked, even though I'd never done anything like it before. My timing was good, I was very lucky that I was in London at that time because that was when musical theatre was starting to really take off. Plus, I had a feeling I wasn't prepared to share with anyone other than Clare, that I had to show the world that I could get back up on my feet again, that I wasn't going to disappear without a trace. The hunger that I'd forgotten about, from twenty years ago when I was hunting down jobs, had returned.

I was auditioning for the part of Amos, Roxie Hart's husband. I had the pieces of music, I had the script and I'd seen what the other actors had been doing, those who were also auditioning for it. I knew that what the other actors did for their audition was to get the Musical Director to take them through the piece they were to audition: 'Can you help me, look here's a bottle of Scotch…' I was nervous at first but with the MD's help I managed to get over my fears and the song, 'Mr Cellophane', sounded good after some rehearsals. Although I was on-stage in *The Rocky Horror Show*, the Narrator doesn't sing a solo like that so this was another new venture for me.

Barry came along to my audition with me, I performed my well-rehearsed piece, I was thanked for coming along and that was it. I felt very confident as I went off on tour with *The Rocky Horror Show*. The tour was great and for nine, ten weeks I had a good time on the road with this wonderful company. When that came to an end I went to start rehearsing for the pantomime. *Aladdin* was a whole new thing; I played Wishy-Washy and we were rehearsing at the Old Vic. The Dame there was Bobby Bennett, and I said to Bobby, 'I don't know how to do this, pantomime's new to me. I mean I did it at college but I was just in the band.' He showed me how to perform the role, showed me his technique and some tricks and so by the time I went to Brighton I had a great time. I made a few mistakes, although they weren't too serious and as this was panto I don't think anyone noticed. My stage fright seemed to have left me, thank God.

Then I heard from Barry about *Chicago*: 'You've got it, you open 9th Feb,' he said. The beginning of 2004 was frenzied. I finished *Aladdin* on a Sunday night, then drove back to Manchester, where the next day Katie May (May, after my grandmother) was born. That afternoon I flew back to London and started rehearsing *Chicago*. I didn't know where I was. When rehearsals were over, I walked back to my flat – I'd rented the same one I'd had over the other side of the river before – and sat down. I tried to take stock: I'd left *Coronation Street*, expecting life to be hard as a result, and I'd barely had time to myself since I'd been working so hard. I was the very proud father of a brand new baby daughter and yet I'm sat here, alone, far from my family. I was starting to get nervous about being on stage in *Chicago,* I couldn't seem to remember my lines.

I tried to distract myself by going out to eat, but I found

myself in tears at the table. I was wrecked by my feelings of loneliness and isolation – but the key thing here, the word that saved me, was 'feelings'; in the past, I'd have drowned my feelings in drink. Now, though, I went to an AA meeting in St Martin's Lane and talked about them instead. Meetings like that over the next two weeks or so were a lifesaver to me, I've always valued them as part of my support network. I was also ringing Win a lot as well, asking for her advice. 'You'll be fine,' she kept telling me. I rationalised by saying to myself that I could only deal with what I could deal with.

I had nine days to rehearse in. I'd seen the show and it scared me half to death. A top professional company with fantastic people like Frances Ruffelle – who was very lovely and very experienced. They were all superb. I was scared to death but this is where sobriety really kicked in: there was no point in me whinging on about the situation, I just had to get on with it. Part of me still felt that I was not worthy, and that I was going to be 'found out'.

After the first week of rehearsals I went home for the weekend, and on the Sunday, Dad came to take me to the airport for a flight down south. I remember saying, 'Dad, you're going to have to take me now, because if you don't, I'm not going to go.'

In the evenings, when I was sat on my own, I'd ring friends for someone to chat to and see if any of them had any advice for me. Two days before opening I rang Gary Owen, who'd played for Manchester City and England. I confessed, 'I'm scared, Gary.' Gary gave me a footballer's pep talk for the West End – and it was brilliant. 'They wouldn't have hired you if they didn't think you could do it. Just go out, don't be nervous; you're there because you deserve to be there. So go out there and give it your best. Are you on in the first half?' I mumbled that I was, that I was on stage then but did my main stuff in the second half. 'Go out there for the first half,' he said, 'get yourself accustomed to what's going on, do what you've got to do so the second half, when you go out, then you're going to be alright because there'll be no more surprises.'

That was the best thing he could have said to me; Gary put the whole thing into perspective. I was still very nervous, and as I walked down the Strand to the theatre for my first night on stage, I saw the sign advertising *Chicago* above the Adelphi coming up ahead, and thought, it would be alright if someone stabbed me. Not enough to kill me, just maybe stab me in the legs so I couldn't go on. But I ploughed on and made it to the stage door. Barry was in the audience, he'd called me and said, 'Don't worry about it, it's just your friends out there, willing you to do your best. Don't worry.' He was great.

Once inside, I headed for my dressing room and got made up. I had my mic put on and then walked to the stage. There was a big stand for the band, and two walkways either side brought you on the stage. Once you step forward and make a left turn, there's only one way you're going – out in front of the audience. I stood there, waiting for my moment, and realised my knees were banging together in my trousers. I was terrified. I'd been scared before, scared for my life, but nothing like this… This was it. Abject terror.

There was a white line taped on the floor, and I thought, once I step over that, that's it. Gary's pep talk had got me to that white line. The moment came, I heard my cue, I stepped across and walked very slowly out onto the stage. I got through the first bit and then came off, but I still had my big bit, the solo. I'm on stage on my own, singing my song. There's a full band behind me and around 2,000 people out there in front of me; for some reason, and this happens to me a lot when I've been getting myself wound up before a scene, my knees had calmed down. As I turned round to walk off the stage there was huge applause, the audience cheering and everything. I felt so humble. So exhausted. So amazingly happy. Unlike the other shows I'd done, *Aladdin*, and *The Rocky Horror Show*, this was all me – and when that applause rang out I realised I was on to my own personal next stage, whatever that will be. I was moving forward.

A number of the *Coronation Street* cast came down to see me and that was a special night for me. Clare came down to stay along with Katie, and we took her out to the Ivy. Mum and Dad came to see the show, too. I went on Sky's *Soccer AM* to promote it. I loved being able to say: 'I'm on in the West End *again*' because most people only knew me for being on *Coronation Street*, so it was nice to point out I'd been here before. Although this time it was new, because it was a musical.

I was offered another six months on *Chicago,* but Clare put her foot down and said no. I'd been on the go for eight months non-stop, and she rightly saw that I needed a rest, so we went to Spain together. When we were settled in Spain I went to see a friend of mine who ran a radio station there, and he pointed out that someone was opening a TV station in the building opposite him. I went to talk to the guy, and from those conversations we agreed that I'd make a TV series for him called *Spanish Capers*, which ran there for over a year. The series involved me travelling around Spain, trying out local tasty food, watching bull runs, meeting girls, going to Ibiza, driving all over the place in a Morgan sports car, meeting girls, jumping off cliffs, meeting girls… it was great fun to make and we made two series in the end. I popped back to England to do pantomimes, one in Nottingham, one in Portsmouth, which kept me in touch with my agent there so I was able to be cast in another musical, this time as the Child Catcher in *Chitty Chitty Bang Bang*.

The Child Catcher isn't the biggest part but it's very important in the play, and of course very memorable, most children of a certain age will tell you the Child Catcher gave them nightmares when they were little. We were touring, covering Manchester and Birmingham. Sharing the role of the lead, Caractacus Potts, was Brian Conley (for three months), and then Gary Wilmot took over. I watched Brian and Gary play this part and I thought they were the finest musical stars we have in this country, they both made it look effortless. It's one of the biggest roles in musical theatre, Caractacus Potts is on stage all the way through, and even when you've got to the end of Act One you've got the song and dance 'Old Bamboo' to do. I thought I could do that too, and one day I summoned up the courage, to tell Brian that I thought I could do that, and cheaper than him, too. Brian didn't laugh in my face, which was something. He was very encouraging: 'The first thing you've got to do,' he said, 'is to get your eyes sorted out. You can't go on with glasses and contact lenses are a pain in the arse.' He'd had his eyes fixed and told me it made a marvellous difference. It was amazing to me when I finally had the operation done; it involved my eyes being cut open and new lenses inserted, so it wasn't something you do on a whim, but it worked for me. It was fantastic after wearing glasses for so long and not having to think where they are, or pick them up off the floor after Katie had batted them away from my face.

Denise Welch came to see the show with her kids. They came to the dressing room and saw me put my Child Catcher make-up on; I gave them a false nose each. Before then, Clare and I had decided to try IVF one more time and we had a second daughter, Gracie, who was born in the same room as Katie. As the show was in Manchester, it meant I was not only there for the birth, but also able to be around all of my family for three months. The night after Gracie was born I was back on stage, and at curtain call that night while I was still in costume, Brian announced, 'Ladies and Gentlemen, I have to tell you, Kevin Kennedy here, who plays the Child Catcher, had another daughter today, her name's Grace.' We all laughed as there was a big round of applause for me – the Child Catcher – taking a bow for the birth of a child!

I did get to play Caractacus Potts, and it was in the unlikeliest of places – Singapore. I was asked to audition for the show; as *Chitty Chitty Bang Bang* was written by Ian Fleming, the producers were also the producers of the James Bond films. When I heard from Barry that I'd got the part, I rang Clare: 'Hey! Call me Caractacus.' Although I have to be honest and admit that the best part of any job is when your agent tells you you've got it; after that it's all downhill because then you've actually got to do it. Clare and I had agreed that she and the girls would fly out to see me in the show. Clare thought it would be too expensive for all of us, but I thought the memory would last longer than any debt.

We had two weeks rehearsing in Southampton, where all the kit was being readied for shipping to Singapore, then five weeks off before flying out and rehearsing for one more week. This was my first big lead. After the initial fortnight, I'd not rehearsed it for five weeks. I was supposed to fly out on the Tuesday, and couldn't remember it all, just bits and pieces of the songs and dance routines. It was a nightmare. When I rehearse, I don't really put everything into it, I'm marking out my movements on stage, my emphasis on my lines, what I do when I go there – when I get in front of an audience it's a different thing. Some of the actors knew what I was doing but from others there were a few mumbles: He's not going to do it like that is he? A bit underplayed? A bit TV? Our flights were postponed, for me to rehearse some more – I took this very personally, and was very upset. I rang Win, who thought I'd gone back to drinking again I was so upset. I said, 'I feel like I've let everyone down, what am I going to do?' She told me to relax, to go home and spend time with the family. I worked hard for three solid days, a crash course in how to play a lead. I rehearsed with Gillian Lynne, a legendary choreographer, responsible for *Cats* and *Phantom of the Opera* among other things. I told her, 'I am not a West End dancer, I am an actor.' She replied,

'Darling, start strongly, finish strongly, and they'll never notice the bit in the middle.' She has a fearsome reputation but she was absolutely lovely with me and we had such fun. By the time it came for me to fly, I was ready.

I slept all the way to Singapore, I was so exhausted. I shared an apartment with Jaymz Denning, a big Scottish actor and he helped me with my lines, by playing all the parts; together we'd sit by the pool in 40 degree heat while he read out the lines for Truly Scrumptious, and I tried not to laugh. Richard O'Brien, who wrote *The Rocky Horror Show*, was playing the Child Catcher, and he lay beside us in some sort of mankini.

Eventually everything was ready. I start the show forty foot up, on a window cleaning machine, and then I had to whoosh right across the stage, doing a big number, 'Jeremy! Jemima! And my name is...' I thought I was scared doing *Chicago* – I cannot tell you the level of fear I felt before the curtain rose. The moment arrived and, as before, a sense of calm came over me, I don't know where from. You're here now, it's too late, let's just get on with it. I cranked the wheel, the thing swung out in front of 2,000 people 12,000 miles from home, and off I went.

That night, after we'd taken the curtain call, everyone went off partying, I went to a Ben & Jerry's and bought myself a huge tub of ice cream and walked down to Raffles hotel. There was a bench outside, I plonked myself down and ate my ice cream surrounded by wonderful tropical evening heat. That was something really special, a treat just for myself, to be sat in this amazing place, watching the people coming in and out of the hotel, with my ice cream. I'd actually done it. I realised I will never be frightened of anything ever again. I'd never done that amount of singing before but it went really well and that gave me the confidence to think I could do more on stage back home. It didn't even cross my mind to go and join the party. I wanted that moment to myself, it was special.

Every evening after the show we would wander the streets, Singapore is an amazing city. We'd sit on the pavement and watch the English Premier League, keeping up with Manchester City whatever time of day we liked, in our shorts because of the heat, eating lovely cheap food. The girls flew out for Christmas, and we all had a wonderful time – what's not to like, Daddy's got a flying car and is Mr Music – before it sadly came to an end.

After a short break while the set was shipped back to the UK, we opened at the Alhambra in Bradford, where I was reunited with Ken Morley who was playing Baron Bomburst. There are some people that bring out the worst in you, and Ken Morley is one of those people. When I'm with him, I regress to about six years of age; any bodily function becomes really funny. This was the first time I'd acted with him in ten years and despite all of the progress

I had made within the theatre, the moment I was reunited with Ken I quickly reverted to this foul-mouthed giggling wreck. It was one of the happiest times in my life.

Ken and I formed a fearful triple act when we were joined for the performances in Bradford by Tony Adams (who had played Adam Chance in *Crossroads*). Tony was cast as Grandpa Potts, and the three of us had dressing rooms next to each other. Tony – who's a lovely man and very, very proper – also regressed to the age of six, and we would shout out our banter so loudly from room to room that people would come to gawk at the noise. We shared a dresser that we called Strumpet – Strumpet, where's me trousers! became our catchphrase. It was great fun, but then about three-quarters of the way through the run I fell ill.

My psoriasis had started to come back, but this time it was a lot worse, and my voice started to go. For the first time ever I had to say I couldn't do the show – I still had this belief that if I couldn't do the show then they were going to find someone else and I'd never be back on stage again – so I carried on when I shouldn't have. I'd become erythrodermic, where the skin all over my body failed. Skin is the biggest organ in the body, so essentially it's organ failure. I'd had two auditions, one for *Spamalot* and one for *Casualty*. I went to a hotel near the theatre and I took all my clothes off, covered myself in paraffin ointment – the stuff put on burns victims – and waited for it to dry before I could get dressed. Once I was ready, I then went to the audition. I got through to the next round for *Spamalot*, which meant I had to go back to the hotel to stay the night in London.

The job for *Casualty* was to play a dying man. Again I had to go through the same routine, I had to find a hotel room and cover myself in this thick ointment. I did the audition but Barry told me I didn't get the part, apparently I looked too ill to play a dying man. It was just as well as the next day I was admitted to hospital, and spent the next six weeks there.

I didn't think that falling ill had anything to do with my drinking, illness is just illness after all. I don't blame alcohol, God or other people – it was my fault or error or whatever, and I had to deal with it. This is what I was missing before. This is what I learned in recovery; the tools I'd learned were for moments like this, when things were thrown in my way. Recovery had taught me acceptance, and I am glad of that. If I hadn't had that serenity then all the things I'd faced – unable to have children, losing my job, falling seriously ill – would have all been triggers for me to go and get leathered. All I was worried about was how I was going to provide for my family.

My first outing back on stage was another panto, this time with Jade Goody in Lincoln. I wasn't quite well but I had to work. Jade had been diagnosed with cancer and it certainly put my worries into perspective. Initially I'd been quite snobbish about working with Jade. I'd read all the articles written about her, and I wondered what I was doing working with a reality TV star. How wrong was I because she turned out to be an absolutely beautiful girl, who, even though she hadn't had any training for what she was doing on stage, never let anyone down because she gave her everything. She had to undergo chemotherapy during the day, and then drive up to Lincoln and perform at night. I cannot praise Jade highly enough. There are not enough superlatives to use for her resilience, her will. To see this girl who had so much to live for, her boys and her mum and Jeff, made my skin problems pale into insignificance. It was very sad. It was the time when my girls learned what death is all about because they'd seen Jade in rehearsal, they'd seen her perform, and when she died there was press everywhere. I had to explain to them that she was poorly and died. That was a very sad time. It was very strange to do this panto, with kids laughing and families enjoying themselves, with this girl literally dying as we worked.

One person I could help was Denise Welch, who had come to me to discuss the problems she'd faced with alcohol. She had said, 'There were mornings when I can't tell you how hard it was to get up for work, and then, when I was on the set, I felt I couldn't say a line properly. I would watch an episode I'd been in and would hardly remember doing it.' I gladly showed her where to go. I didn't become her mentor; I told her what had happened to me, and helped her deal with it. She's still in recovery (at the point of writing) and I wish her all the best.

Meanwhile, Barry put me up for another audition, this time for the Queen musical written by Ben Elton, *We Will Rock You* at the Dominion Theatre. I was to play the part of Pop. I'd rehearsed the song with Ged, 'These Are The Days Of Our Lives'. I said, 'If I get this gig, Ged, you're coming to the first night.' I auditioned in front of the director and casting director and told them before I began how I felt about the part: 'I want to do it differently from this hippy bloke, I want him to have a bit of attitude. More like a Mancunian or a Liverpudlian. If I can name the person I want Pop to be like he'd be Frank Gallagher from TV's *Shameless*.' Sometimes saying that you want to do things differently from the way they currently are portrayed can be the kiss of death in an audition. Not this time, though, they liked what I did with the role, and asked me back for a second audition. The following week I walked in and there were so many people, I've never seen so many at an audition. Along with the director and casting director I'd met before, there was Mike Dixon, a Musical Director who has his name on almost everything in the West End, and, just in case that wasn't enough, two men I didn't need introducing to: Ben Elton and Brian May. I was terrified, I didn't know they were all going to be there. I managed to do my stuff, I sang my song and felt happy with the way it had gone. 'Thank you very much for coming in, we'll let you know.' I had gone to get some lunch when Barry called. 'They want you to go back again.' My answer was simply: 'Well I'm not going until I've finished these sausages.'

I went back and Brian May explained to me that Roger Taylor – who wrote the song I'd auditioned with – couldn't be at this audition, and asked if there was any way I could come back tomorrow. I explained that I couldn't, as I was still in the panto then and we had a matinee the next day. After some chin-rubbing and muttered conversations, Brian produced his mobile phone and passed it over to me. Mike Dixon sat behind the piano and I sang the song into the phone for it to be played the next day to Roger. As I walked out I figured it didn't matter if I didn't get the job because I'd be able to dine out on that story for years.

Ben Elton told me he was really impressed with the approach I'd taken. He was the writer of the show and could easily have said to me to act it a certain way, but he didn't. Instead he liked it and said we should develop that. 'You know your way round comedy,' he added, which made me feel about ten feet tall, until Brian May said, 'You've got rock'n'roll bones,' at which point I felt fifty feet tall.

Initially I performed *We Will Rock You* on tour for about a year. Life on the road was different to what I remembered

– people didn't drink to excess, not like in the old days. Or maybe that was just me. After about two months we played in Manchester. One night, Brian and Roger played with us too, so there I was at the Palace Theatre in my home town, on stage with Roger Taylor on drums and Brian May, playing the guitar solo out of 'Bohemian Rhapsody' as an encore on a VOX AC30 just like my old one. I thought, I'm from Wythenshawe, what am I doing here? At the age of fifty I found myself with long hair rocking out with one of the most incredible rock bands the world has ever known with girls screaming and waving at me. What more could anyone ask for?

The answer is, of course, to return to the West End for the fourth time. I'm back in at the Dominion, again playing the role of Pop, which is where I've been performing it now since September 2010. I'm still ambitious; I'm still improving as an actor. I watch the younger members of the cast and I learn off them. I'm always learning. Clare and the girls moved south, and we now live in Brighton. I've settled into a bit of a routine; as soon as I finish the show, I take my wig and my make-up off very quickly, put my coat on, slip out through the stage door and suddenly I'm anonymous again. I love the euphoria I feel on stage, but I no longer crave it the way I did when I was younger, the way I think I tried to prolong that by drinking. Now I feel I'm doing what I'm supposed to be doing. I feel like I fit in. Like I'm actually achieving everything I should and can do. I get back home late, so the girls are all asleep; I'll tiptoe in and kiss them goodnight. I'll slip any change in my pockets into the dinner money bowl by the front door for school; I make a sandwich, and watch whatever's on the History channel. Even better if it's a Saturday night and there's Match of the Day.

My sister's now teaching radiography at Liverpool University and Mum and Dad are now both retired. They are still going strong and dote on our two children, Grace and Katie.

I don't know what happened to my old friends. I don't miss the drinking buddies, because I don't miss drinking, but I miss my old school friends. I saw Michael Galway at my gran's funeral, and I see his mum and dad now at football matches. You never have friends like those you've got when you're fourteen. You have no guile at that stage – you just want to get up and run around all day, kicking a ball, or pointing a stick. You go through the shared experiences of school.

I loved being Curly, how could I not? I was very lucky because I got to play so many different aspects of this character – the mad-cap stuff at one hundred miles an hour, with props everywhere to play with like food, sandwiches, tea, as there was always tea. Sedate, gentle comedy with Emily, slapstick with the Duckworths and mad stuff with

Ken. As an actor, it allowed me to hone all my skills.

I've found it very painful writing about my time as an alcoholic. It's an area I've chosen not to revisit very often. I thought it would be like writing about something that happened in another time, to another person, but I'd forgotten – to a certain extent, which is both good and bad – about the grip that the addiction had on me. And how I managed to pretend it was so normal. I know the differences between good and bad, right and wrong, but the brain is an incredible thing, it convinced me there was a huge grey area where I could justify what I was doing. I found myself manipulating myself and everyone else to get what I wanted. Denial is so strong that it convinced even me, who, as the one living that life, should have known better.

I've been sober a long time now, and my story is one of redemption, of overcoming adversity. For anyone reading this who needs to hear this message, I'll say it again; you don't have to drink again. I've now been sober for fifteen years. Sometimes it feels more like fifteen minutes, though, as so much has happened to me since then. The first one I'd note is that I'm still alive, which is a fantastic gift. I stayed with *Coronation Street* and was part of some of the show's biggest developments. Clare and I have two beautiful children, when we thought we couldn't have any. I was signed by Simon Cowell. I became a musical theatre star, back in the West End. My life's not perfect, but my problems are not enlarged through the bottom of a glass. I can deal with them. I have no Devil to fear. I go to meetings and we discuss everything, systematically taking the horns off the Devil. All the demons we all suffered from were taken apart in the meetings. This is how our meetings worked. When a newcomer arrived, we'd all get a sense of how far we'd progressed – and the newcomers could see how far they could go, away from their problems, if they put the time and energy in. People would exchange phone numbers and sometimes the strongest work was done outside the meetings, but when people are in a room like that and baring their souls, a bond is formed. There's a trust there and you can say what you want and it won't go any further. That's amazing. Especially in today's world. But we all understood that for the group to work, we had to stick by the rule – that what you see in here, what you hear in here, stays in here.

A really important feature of our meetings was that they were non-judgemental as well. We could have wasted hours, days, or weeks talking about why we weren't like each other, but we were taught to look for the similarities in our stories. It's that which supported us all. We were all survivors, and we all knew we should have been dead. When I first got sober, I'd never been to so many funerals in my life. Some people can't get sober, they just don't like it. Death was more prevalent amongst that group at that stage than it normally is in society. None of us felt we'd escaped it, we knew we'd worked to get where we were, but we also knew we had to help keep each other on track, to avoid that fate.

I've told my girls that drink used to make Daddy sick, and they know that it is bad for me. I don't know if they'll drink like I did, or if they'll be able to pick it up and put it down again. I hope they'll be sensible with it, but that's up to them. If I prohibit it, it'll only be fascinating and dangerous, and I don't want that. I hope they'll have a healthy respect for it.

As for Dawn and Ryan, I did make contact again and always tried to fulfil my moral as well as my financial obligations, but this did not go well. A clean and sober Kevin is a very different person to the man I was before. I can honestly say to myself and to the world that I tried but I will not be manipulated and lied to. Just because you're in recovery doesn't mean you're a doormat.

Musically I didn't listen to anything between 1985 and 1995 because I thought it was all rubbish. I craved guitar bands and thankfully Oasis and their like came along. I still play with The Borderline now and again although tinged with sadness as Brendan our lead singer died in 2006. I miss him and think of him often.

Getting sober hasn't made me perfect. I still want things, I'm still unreasonable, I still get frustrated. I was one of those who thought the grass was always greener on the other side, that the meal, the pub, the party, the job, the play that I *wasn't* enjoying or going to or working at was better. In the old days I'd have let that get to me, but now I know that's me, I've learned to accept myself for what I am. Driving to the station to take the train into town for work, I go along the road next to the beach. Some mornings the sun shines down on the water and turns the sea into a carpet of silver, sparkling and alive. I stop my car and sit and stare happily – I'd never have found the time to do that before. Now I can see there are beautiful things all around me.

As to the future, well, I'm enjoying the moment now in a way I never did before. Will Curly be seen in Weatherfield? Will Rovers Return?

If it doesn't happen, well, that's life. If it does, then no-one will be happier than me.